Police Misconduct Compl
Investigations Manual

The Police Misconduct Complaint Investigations Manual provides a timely and unique, step-by-step approach to conducting or reviewing police misconduct investigations, whether a complaint involves a lower level allegation of discourtesy or more serious concerns such as excessive force or criminal behavior. Utilizing real-life examples and updated case law to illustrate points, it provides best practices for investigating police action resulting in misconduct complaints. The *Manual*'s comprehensive approach includes detailed procedures and policy considerations from intake through case closure, and discusses data tracking, reporting on trends, selecting and training investigative staff, civilian oversight, and a host of special issues that can arise with police misconduct complaints.

The *Manual* is suitable for both sworn personnel and civilians handling or reviewing investigations and whether working internally for a police department or externally in oversight or another capacity. The guidance provides detailed examples of witness interview questions and types of evidence to collect, with discussion on making difficult credibility determinations and approaches to analyzing the information gathered to arrive at a recommended finding. Review questions are found at the end of most chapters, for use in academic or investigative training environments. Police officers engaged in the often complex and challenging work of public safety deserve and expect objective, thorough, and timely handling of complaints. Complainants and other stakeholders seek accountability and transparency when an officer behaves in a way that raises questions about their professionalism. The *Complaint Investigations Manual* provides instruction on handling misconduct complaints in a manner that will ensure the goals of law enforcement and stakeholders are met.

The authors intentionally use a broad approach to make the *Manual* relevant and easy to use by law enforcement personnel, civilians in oversight or other capacities who work on police misconduct matters, and the criminal justice academic community. It is a critical primer for internal affairs investigators, police managers, law enforcement leaders, auditing professionals, civilian oversight practitioners, government representatives, community advocates, criminal and social justice students, and all others in pursuit of fair, thorough, and timely investigations of police misconduct complaints.

Barbara Attard and Kathryn Olson are leaders in the development of civilian oversight and consultants who specialize in police accountability and transparency. Each has served as president of the National Association for Civilian Oversight of Law Enforcement and have many years of experience managing the complaint investigation process.

Barbara Attard, a police practices consultant at Accountability Associates, has held executive positions in a variety of oversight agencies conducting quality control of police misconduct investigations. Throughout her career she has developed and conducted training on investigations, oversight, ethics, report writing, and community engagement in the United States and internationally. With a focus on accountability systems that ensure fairness and transparency, Barbara's work includes consulting on development of independent oversight programs, providing expert witness testimony, and authoring publications on oversight and mediation.

Kathryn Olson, a partner in Change Integration Consulting, LLC, has deep and broad experience in law, executive leadership, and training, which combine to create a unique skill set to assess practices that impact law enforcement professionals and the communities served. She brings an extensive background in conducting investigations of complex, sensitive complaints in unionized environments, along with personnel and operations management experience, in co-authoring the *Police Misconduct Complaint Investigations Manual*. Kathryn's diverse consulting practice includes handling complaints against police commanders, evaluating investigation systems and developing improvement strategies, and serving as an expert witness on investigation best practices and procedural justice.

Routledge Series on Practical and Evidence-Based Policing

Books in the Routledge Series on Practical and Evidence-Based Policing disseminate knowledge and provide practical tools for law enforcement leaders and personnel to protect and serve the public and reduce crime. With an aim to bridge the "translation gap" between frontline policing and academic research, books in this series apply sound scientific methods as well as practical experience to make everyday police work safer and smarter. These books are an invaluable resource for police practitioners, academic researchers, public policymakers, and students in law enforcement and criminology programs to guide best practices in all aspects of policing.

Police Misconduct Complaint Investigations Manual, 2nd Edition
Barbara Attard and Kathryn Olson

Police Misconduct Complaint Investigations Manual

Second Edition

Barbara Attard and Kathryn Olson

NEW YORK AND LONDON

Second edition published 2021
by Routledge
52 Vanderbilt Avenue, New York, NY 10017

and by Routledge
2 Park Square, Milton Park, Abingdon, Oxon, OX14 4RN

Routledge is an imprint of the Taylor & Francis Group, an informa business

First edition published by Olson & Attard Publishing 2016

Cover photo by Janice Tong, JT Designs

Library of Congress Cataloging-in-Publication Data
Names: Attard, Barbara, author. | Olson, Kathryn
(Police accountability advocate), author.
Title: Police misconduct complaint investigations manual /
Barbara Attard & Kathryn Olson.
Description: Second edition. | New York, NY : Routledge, 2020. |
Includes bibliographical references and index.
Identifiers: LCCN 2020002883 (print) | LCCN 2020002884 (ebook) |
ISBN 9780367405083 (hardback) | ISBN 9780367404352 (paperback) |
ISBN 9780429356452 (ebook)
Subjects: LCSH: Police misconduct—United States. | Police—
Compaints against—United States. | Investigations—United States—
Handbooks, manuals, etc. | Police administration—United States—
Evaluation—Handbooks, manuals, etc.
Classification: LCC HV8141 .A88 2020 (print) | LCC HV8141 (ebook) |
DDC 363.25/932—dc23
LC record available at https://lccn.loc.gov/2020002883
LC ebook record available at https://lccn.loc.gov/2020002884

ISBN: 978-0-367-40508-3 (hbk)
ISBN: 978-0-367-40435-2 (pbk)
ISBN: 978-0-429-35645-2 (ebk)

Typeset in Bembo
by codeMantra

We dedicate the *Manual* to our families for their support and patience.

Contents

Acknowledgments

Kathryn Olson and Barbara Attard are indebted to all of the people, both civilian and sworn, who over the years have contributed to their understanding of the many elements important to timely, objective, and thorough investigations of police misconduct complaints.

Preface to the Second Edition

An earlier version of the *Police Misconduct Complaint Investigations Manual* was published in 2016, with an intended audience of civilian oversight practitioners. The earlier version was designed to provide a tutorial of practices and procedures for those in oversight investigating, reviewing, monitoring, or auditing police misconduct complaints. While the first edition was well received, feedback from law enforcement and criminal justice academic communities indicated that it would be useful to broaden the approach of the *Manual*, to make it more relevant to anyone working with police misconduct complaints, including those interested in studying this facet of the criminal justice system.

This edition of the *Complaint Investigations Manual* is written from the perspective that misconduct allegations in different jurisdictions are handled internally as well as externally, by both sworn and civilian personnel. The term "investigative office" is used throughout to refer to any setting where police misconduct complaints are investigated or reviewed for quality control or to make final determinations. The individual alleging misconduct is referred to as the "complainant," while the person alleged to have engaged in misconduct is called the "named officer" or "subject officer." In referring to law enforcement, terms used are "police department" or "law enforcement" and "police officer" or "law enforcement officer." However, the principles discussed equally apply to investigations of complaints against non-sworn employees in law enforcement, as well as deputies, troopers, and other sworn members of organizations such as sheriff's offices, state patrol agencies, and college or university police departments. While there are unique issues associated with custodial settings, the basic investigative techniques covered in the *Manual* are useful in handling complaints against correctional or detention officers and others working in prisons and jails.

Civilian oversight is mentioned at relevant points throughout the *Manual*, with a larger discussion about the role of oversight in Chapter 9. Finally, discussion questions have been added at the end of most chapters to facilitate review of the material in academic or investigative training contexts.

Chapter 1

Introduction

There has been an increasingly intense focus on policing in the United States as the public has been exposed to more frequent video recordings of law enforcement activities and angered by what is perceived to be misuse of force disproportionately directed at people of color. High profile videotaped police incidents have led to changes on the local level, as was seen with the response to the severe beating of Rodney King in 1991, and demands for more systemic reforms nationwide following the homicide of George Floyd in 2020.

POLICE KILLING OF GEORGE FLOYD — A CALL FOR TRANSFORMATION

On May 25, 2020, George Floyd, a 46-year-old African American man, was killed by Minneapolis Police Officer Derek Chauvin. Bystander video reveals Officer Chauvin kneeling on Mr. Floyd's neck for nearly eight minutes, ignoring his repeated pleas that he could not breathe, as several other officers at the scene failed to stop the misuse of force. Though all of the officers involved were terminated and criminally charged, their apparent disregard for Mr. Floyd's life caused unprecedented protests in all fifty states and around the world, renewing the call for police reform and demanding racial justice.

While Mr. Floyd's homicide was one of many troubling police incidents, his death prompted long overdue discussion and legislation seeking systemic change on federal, state, and local levels to broadly transform law enforcement and address racial inequities in our society. A subsequent federal executive order addressed use of force training, mandated a national database to track police officers who use excessive force, and stated that appropriate social services should be the primary responders for individuals with impaired mental health, homelessness, and addiction. Discussions continued on other potential reforms ranging from a call to defund the police to adoption of a national use of force standard emphasizing the sanctity of life and the need for police response proportional to the threat encountered, implicit bias training, changes in the role of police unions, enforcement of police peer-intervention requirements, a ban on chokeholds and carotid restraints, eradication of the qualified immunity doctrine, and increased law enforcement transparency and accountability.

While there is optimism that changes to law, policy, and training resulting from George Floyd's death will serve to improve policing, all departments nonetheless require a reliable system to investigate and address the full range of problematic interactions that can occur.

The *Police Misconduct Complaint Investigations Manual* (*Complaint Investigations Manual* or *Manual*) is a resource to ensure a law enforcement department has a strong investigations program, helping to build trust and legitimacy between law enforcement and the communities served. Police officers and others engaged in the often complex and challenging work of public safety deserve and expect objective, thorough, and timely handling of complaints. The community and other stakeholders seek accountability and transparency when an officer behaves in a way that raises questions about their professionalism and commitment to constitutional policing. The *Complaint Investigations Manual* provides detailed guidance on handling misconduct complaints, to ensure the goals of both law enforcement and stakeholders are met.

The *Manual* provides detailed information about the range of misconduct complaints involving law enforcement, the stages of complaint handling and investigation, and information about substantive and procedural complaint issues associated with policing. Although officers are found to have acted within policy in the majority of misconduct complaints, the *Manual* advocates for reviewing issues and events underlying allegations during the investigation process to consider whether there are lessons to be learned or policy revisions to be made. The important work of educating stakeholders,

THE RODNEY KING CASE—THE NEED FOR REFORM, INCLUDING CHANGES TO THE COMPLAINT INVESTIGATION AND DISCIPLINE SYSTEMS

Bystander video footage of the stop, beating, and arrest of Rodney King in Los Angeles in 1991 was viewed by many millions of people and caused the incident to rise to national notoriety. A year later, after the Los Angeles Police Department (LAPD) officers involved were acquitted in the first trial, Los Angeles exploded into mass rioting, resulting in over 50 deaths, ten at the hands of law enforcement.[1] After Rodney King's beating, the Independent Commission on the LAPD (Christopher Commission) was formed to examine the department's structure and organization.[2]

The Christopher Commission addressed a wide range of issues, from excessive use of force and racism to recruitment, training, and promotion of officers, to the need for community policing. Of particular relevance here are the deficiencies in complaint handling and discipline that were highlighted by the Christopher Commission, including:

- Inadequate division-assigned investigations, with many investigators failing to locate or interview independent witnesses.
- Serious flaws in the investigation of shooting cases, with officers frequently interviewed as a group, and statements often not recorded until completion of a "pre-interview."
- An investigation system skewed against complainants.
- Discipline leniency for excessive use of force, compared to other sustained matters.

The Christopher Commission's report recommended numerous changes to address these problems, and required that all misuse of force complaints be investigated by internal affairs and that periodic audits of the unit be conducted. The Rodney King incident and its aftermath provide a compelling lesson emphasizing the importance of establishing strong accountability measures that include objective and thorough complaint investigations and an effective discipline system.

reporting on the work of the investigative office, and organizational issues such as personnel selection and training also are addressed. Finally, as many jurisdictions have adopted civilian oversight as a means to bring the community's voice to policing practices, the role of oversight in the misconduct investigation process is discussed.

Throughout this edition of the *Manual* the authors illustrate aspects of the complaint investigation process through references to high profile incidents, likely familiar to the reader without a full discussion of all the attendant facts. The use of widely publicized events to put the principles of the *Complaint Investigations Manual* into context is not intended to minimize the seriousness or complexity of issues involved, including devastating impacts on families and communities, as well as on law enforcement. Taking this into account, the Rodney King incident exemplifies mandated changes for a police department that ignores the requirement for constitutional use of force and devalues the role of the complaint investigation and discipline system to help ensure integrity in enforcement actions.

Notes

1 Anjuli Sastry and Karen Grigsby Bates, "When LA Erupted in Anger: A Look Back at the Rodney King Riots," *NPR Special Series: The Los Angeles Riots, 25 Years On* (April 26, 2017).

2 *Report of the Independent Commission on the Los Angeles Police Department* (1991), http://michellawyers.com/wp-content/uploads/2010/06/Report-of-the-Independent-Commission-on-the-LAPD-re-Rodney-King_Reduced.pdf

In Chapter 2

Complaint Intake and the Initial Assessment Process

A. Is This the Proper Place to Resolve the Complaint?
B. Administrative Complaints—Intake Process
   1. Accepting Misconduct Complaints
   2. Types of Allegations Raised in Misconduct Complaints
   3. Conducting the Intake Interview
   4. Establishing Officer Identification
   5. Developing an Investigative Plan
   6. Conducting the Preliminary Investigation
   7. Preliminary Steps for Investigating Allegations of Bodily Injury
C. Defining Allegations and Assessing the Underlying Incident for Additional Claims
D. Investigative Timelines, Communicating with Complainants and Officers, and Complaint Tracking
   1. Investigative Timelines
   2. Communicating with Complainants and Officers
   3. Tracking Systems
E. Mediation/Alternative Dispute Resolution Options

Chapter 2

Complaint Intake and the Initial Assessment Process

Police misconduct complaints serve as a valuable quality control, risk management tool for law enforcement agencies, providing a perspective of officer conduct in the field that might not otherwise be available to supervisors and commanders. Timely, thorough, and objective investigations are important to the complainant and officer involved, as well as the police agency and larger community. Even complaints that are not sustained may provide insight into community concerns or suggest training opportunities. All complaints must be properly evaluated, classified, and investigated in a timely manner, with findings and discipline tracked systematically to ensure accurate record keeping and facilitate reporting on complaint trends.

COMPLAINT INVESTIGATION OVERVIEW

- Appropriate agency determination
- Intake and preliminary investigation
- Identification of allegations and complaint classification
- Notice of complaint
- Investigation
- Summarization of evidence, recommended findings, and any policy/training recommendations in investigative report
- Review and determination of findings
- Implementation of discipline for sustained findings and follow through on policy/training recommendations, if any
- Complaint closure, notification to parties, and data entry

A. Is This the Proper Place to Resolve the Complaint?

When a misconduct complaint is received, a determination must be made as to whether it involves a matter that should be handled by the investigative office or referred elsewhere, at least initially. Issues stemming from alleged police misconduct are resolved through several distinct processes. When appropriate, personnel handling intake should provide information about the different types of action that can be taken to address the complainant's grievances:

- Administrative Investigations
  - Administrative investigations are conducted for the purpose of determining whether or not an officer engaged in misconduct that could result in disciplinary or other action. Federal and

state law govern police conduct, and law enforcement agencies have internal policies, procedures, and other operational directives that further set specific conduct expectations. Investigative offices investigate or review allegations related to such internal policies, procedures, and directives.

- Criminal Investigations
  - Complaints involving questionable use of force or other potential violations of criminal law should be referred to either the law enforcement agency criminal investigations unit or a prosecutor who can ensure an investigation is conducted. Procedures should be developed for handling administrative issues in cases that also involve investigations of criminal allegations against officers. See Chapter 5.C. for more information.
- Civil Lawsuits
  - Complainants alleging misconduct may be seeking monetary damages or other relief against an officer or law enforcement agency under state or federal law. A referral to the proper office within the jurisdiction that considers monetary claims against the department and personnel should be made. The investigative office should independently evaluate the misconduct allegations to determine if an administrative investigation should be initiated, even if the complainant is also pursuing a civil claim. See Chapter 5.B. for more information.

B. Administrative Complaints—Intake Process

Intake procedures should be established to facilitate the filing of complaints, assess the seriousness of the allegations involved, and appropriately classify and investigate misconduct allegations. The goal is to ensure prompt, effective, and efficient handling of all communications and complaints.

Whether or not issues raised are to be further investigated, it is important to have a means to record all contacts. Even when individuals raise questions or request information unrelated to a complaint, the contact should be recorded and tracked. A brief summary of all contacts provides information about how the public is reaching out to the investigative office, and becomes useful if questions arise down the line about how a matter was handled or if someone is making chronic, unsubstantiated complaints. Complaints that develop into full investigations will need to be tracked in more detail, to ensure timely and thorough processing and allow for statistical analysis of issues and complaint trends.

Given that an investigative office typically will be contacted about a variety of matters that do not fall within its jurisdiction, and complainants can raise issues not directly related to a police incident, a ready list of resources for referrals is useful. The list should be regularly reviewed and updated, and made available to all investigative office personnel.

HANDLING HIGH PROFILE INCIDENTS

point of contact? Q

A high profile incident can result in many people contacting the investigative office to complain about the same police event. Protocols should be established to log all such related complaints as appropriate, without necessarily initiating separate investigations.

1. Accepting Misconduct Complaints

To promote a culture that fosters accountability and builds trust with the community served, the law enforcement agency and the investigative office must clearly communicate a commitment to resolving all concerns raised through the complaint process. Toward that end, complaints should be accepted by whatever means they are communicated, whether in person, by phone, voicemail or email, through the agency's website, via letter, or other means. To the extent permitted by jurisdictional authority, complaints should be accepted regardless of who is initiating or filing the complaint, including but not limited to the subject of a police incident, a witness, a juvenile, a third party (such as the parent or spouse of the subject), a legal representative, an anonymous person, and anyone aware of the incident, including government officials and referral agencies. Allowing anonymous complaints enables persons who may not feel comfortable providing their names, such as undocumented immigrants afraid of deportation, or others fearing retaliation, to register grievances.

> **COMPLAINT VERIFICATION**
>
> Some jurisdictions require that the complainant sign the complaint to verify its truthfulness. While such a requirement is aimed at preventing spurious allegations of misconduct, it can have the negative effect of deterring people from bringing forth legitimate concerns. Also, requiring truthfulness verification is not compatible with accepting anonymous complaints or complaints from representatives, such as parents, filing on behalf of a complainant.

In some jurisdictions, the investigative office has authority to initiate investigations under specified circumstances. For example, where a confidential source provides substantive information concerning an incident of misconduct, but declines to file a complaint, the investigative office may have the authority to pursue an investigation on its own initiative.

2. Types of Allegations Raised in Misconduct Complaints

Administrative complaints can range from concerns about relatively minor transgressions to allegations of serious misbehavior, all of which are considered in light of the law enforcement agency's conduct expectations. Most police departments have general orders or a policy manual, often available on-line, which mandates rules and procedures that officers are expected to follow to ensure their conduct is professional and meets legal standards and community expectations. Allegations raised in complaints vary widely, and may include concerns about an employee's attitude or discourteous behavior, service quality, misuse of force, biased policing, decisions related to searches, failure to respond or take action, abuse of discretion, criminal violations, failure to follow video or other recording protocols, or a myriad of other issues related to on- or off-duty conduct. It is important to clearly understand the types of allegations the investigative office has

COMPLAINTS THAT MAY REQUIRE PRIORITIZATION

Complaint procedures should include directives for special handling of certain cases. Factors to consider include:

- The need to obtain or document perishable evidence—surveillance camera video may be erased or recorded over within a short time, physical injuries can heal if not photographed while visible, or witnesses may become unavailable or be more difficult to locate as time passes.
- The time that has elapsed between the incident and the filing of the complaint—the more time that has passed, the more difficult it can be to prove or disprove allegations, and such cases might be considered for lower priority, unless they are particularly serious or involve criminal issues.
- The potential for media coverage or other information sources to impact or shape witnesses' recollections—moving more quickly to take witnesses' statements may be advisable in high profile cases to collect testimony before it is influenced by accounts in the media or where there is concern a witness might retract their statement due to pressure from others.
- The seriousness of the issues involved—complaints involving more serious issues, such as integrity, honesty, or criminal allegations, should be treated with higher priority or referred out if the investigative office does not have the resources necessary to conduct an expeditious investigation.

authority to investigate and to know the appropriate referral options for claims outside of that authority.

Complaints involving criminal allegations against an officer, such as theft of evidence, a questionable shooting, or domestic violence, may require special handling through a prosecuting attorney's office or a specialized police department unit, and can be multi-jurisdictional. If a criminal matter is involved, the administrative investigation might be stayed until the criminal proceeding is concluded; in some jurisdictions, however, the administrative investigation is conducted concurrently. If the administrative investigation is stayed, the investigative office should have a system to track the criminal proceedings and, when appropriate, initiate the administrative investigation. This issue is discussed in Chapter 5.C.

Based on an evaluation of the information available, the complaint must be triaged to determine whether it requires immediate attention or can proceed through routine intake processing. Examples of issues that should be immediately brought to the attention of management include those in which criminal allegations against an officer may be involved, complaints in which there is developing media attention, any complaint against a member of the law enforcement agency command staff or investigative office personnel, and allegations brought by an elected official. If a complaint is brought against investigative office personnel, it may be necessary to refer the matter to another investigative body to avoid any real or perceived conflict of interest.

PENDING CRIMINAL CHARGES

Communications explaining the complaint investigation process should inform any **complainant** facing criminal charges that they may want to consult an attorney before making a formal statement, as that statement may become available to the prosecuting authority and the complainant would be disadvantaged if they self-incriminate in the statement. The attorney may advise the complainant to wait until the criminal case is adjudicated before providing a formal statement, to avoid jeopardizing their defense against the criminal charges.

However, if the investigative office is given information that constitutes notice of misconduct, it may trigger investigative timelines and necessitate that an investigation be initiated. State law, agency policy, or a collective bargaining contract could control whether an investigation can be stayed until criminal charges against the complainant are concluded. Input from the investigative office counsel may be necessary before proceeding.

If the **named officer** is facing criminal charges, they likely will want to confer with their union representative or attorney, as there are potential conflicts between employment obligations in the administrative investigation and legal rights in the criminal case. This issue is discussed in depth in Chapters 3.C.4. and 7.C.3.

3. *Conducting the Intake Interview*

In order to determine if the investigative office has authority to investigate a reported incident, it is usually necessary to conduct an intake interview of the complainant and a preliminary investigation of the facts alleged. Sometimes this initial investigation will be sufficient to determine the merits of the complaint or clarify that the matter should be referred elsewhere for handling. The intake process should identify if any specific allegations require further investigation and point to necessary next steps in the process.

If the complainant submits a written complaint, such as through mail, email, or the agency website, much of the information needed to assess the situation may be gleaned from the written submission. However, an interview of the complainant should always be conducted, if possible, as follow up to a written statement of complaint to ensure thoroughness.

a) General Approach to the Intake Interview

The initial interview of a complainant is an important first step in an investigation and must be conducted properly to ensure accurate documentation of the complaint and delineation of allegations. Taking a complainant's statement in person allows the investigator to assess demeanor, body language, and other nonverbal communication, take pictures if there is a claim of bodily injury, and establish rapport. However, initial contact and discussion of the incident may occur by phone, and the need for another interview in person should be evaluated.

During the intake interview the complainant should be allowed to provide a complete narrative of the complaint. If possible, the investigator conducting the interview should not interrupt with questions unless a minor clarification is necessary to understand the statement. Asking questions can inadvertently direct and change a statement; therefore, questions requesting more in-depth information should be noted and asked after the initial narrative. A full discussion of best practices for conducting interviews is provided in Chapter 3.C.

Investigators should be aware that the complainant may initially sound tentative when making a statement about alleged officer misconduct. There can be many reasons for this hesitancy, from being unfamiliar and insecure about the complaint system to feeling vulnerable about retaliation.

Investigators should handle the interview respectfully, explain the investigative process and prohibitions against retaliation, and explore whether the complainant has other concerns if the hesitancy persists.

Non-fluent English speakers or others may need an interpreter or assistance for their interview. Investigative offices should provide translators or other accommodations as necessary during the intake process, or as otherwise needed to facilitate the testimony of any witness during the investigation. For more information about accessibility, see Chapter 8.A.

RETALIATION SHOULD BE EXPLICITLY PROHIBITED

All law enforcement departments should have a policy encouraging aggrieved parties to file complaints and stating that retaliation against a complainant, witness, or anyone else involved in the matter is impermissible and will not be tolerated.

Throughout the investigation, investigators should watch for indications of retaliation. If appropriate, an allegation of retaliation should be added. Examples of potential retaliation include:

- During the incident, someone asks for an officer's name or badge number and the officer then arrests the person for a discretionary charge when it had appeared earlier that no arrest was going to be made.
- After filing a complaint, the complainant is repeatedly stopped and frisked, though no arrests are made.

Alleged retaliation should be brought to the attention of investigative office management and protocols should be in place to immediately inform police command staff that an allegation of retaliation has been filed. Commanders may choose to reassign the involved officer or take other steps to distance the officer from interactions with the complainant.

b) Covering the Basics in the Intake Interview

Once the complainant has provided a complete narrative of the event, follow-up questions should ensure that basic information about the incident is gathered during the intake interview. While the relevance of different topics depends on the nature of the complaint, sample follow-up issues include:

Who was involved in the incident? Does the complaint involve an officer in the law enforcement agency within the jurisdiction of the investigative office? If the officer's name is known, who established the officer's identity and how was that accomplished? Who was present at the time of the incident or may know something about it? Who are the people involved; i.e., complainants, witnesses, and officers? What is the address, phone number, email address, and/or other contact information for each person involved? If any person involved is transient or homeless, attempt to get a back-up means of contact, such as through a relative, friend, or service agency.

WHAT *What happened?* Obtain a detailed description of the alleged misconduct. Ask about the circumstances prior to, during, and after the event. What was the complainant's involvement? What are the relationships among the involved parties?

WHEN *When did the incident happen?* Obtain the date(s) and time(s) of the alleged misconduct. Was the involved officer on- or off-duty? When and how did the complainant learn of the alleged misconduct, if the complainant is not the subject? If there is a delay in filing a complaint following the incident at issue, ask for an explanation.

WHERE *Where did the incident happen?* Obtain specific information about the location of the incident at issue, including the location of involved parties and witnesses and accessibility of the incident from different vantage points.

WHY *Asking why the incident happened is more complex.* Sometimes it is appropriate to ask why the complainant thinks the officer engaged in the conduct at the heart of the complaint. "Why" questions can prompt responses that might provide facts relevant to proving the misconduct allegation, suggest a new allegation, or point to facts supporting the officer's actions. However, "why" questions also can lead the complainant to speculate about the officer's intentions and actions without any foundation. It is important to consider when to use "why" questions and to separate responsive facts from speculation.

HOW *How did it happen?* How did the officer become involved with the complainant? How can the investigator learn more about the incident? How would the complainant like to see the matter resolved?

The ability to conduct effective interviews is integral to ensuring a thorough assessment of complaints of police misconduct; however, developing interview skills requires training and practice.

c) Recording the Intake Interview

The standard practice is to seek a recorded account from the complainant when initially present or in contact by phone. There are advantages to immediately recording a statement and, for various reasons, this may be the only opportunity to acquire testimony on tape. Obtaining a comprehensive recording at the beginning of the complaint process can speed up the evaluation and investigation of the complaint, and can be useful in assessing credibility if the complainant makes conflicting statements.

The investigator should obtain permission from the complainant to record the interview and note permission on the record. If the complainant (or any witness) refuses to provide a recorded statement for any reason, whether sought during intake or later, make a written note of the reasons a statement was not recorded.

It is advantageous to transcribe all interviews as it makes it easier for the investigator, supervisor, and others to review testimony for missing information or leads on other evidence, and helps in evaluating the overall case. However, transcription is not always feasible, given competing resource demands, though some jurisdictions require that officers be provided a transcribed copy of their interviews to review for accuracy. See Chapter 3.C.6. for information about writing an interview summary when recording or transcription is not possible.

4. Establishing Officer Identification

The identity of the named officer is usually known by the complainant or easy to ascertain, although establishing officer identification can be difficult in some cases, such as an incident that involves numerous officers. Usually there will be a citation, arrest report, video/audio recording, or other police documentation indicating the officer(s) involved in the incident underlying the misconduct complaint. The method of identification used by the investigator should be noted in the file.

If the complainant is not able to name the involved officer(s) and identification is unclear from existing records and recordings, determining an involved officer's identity will be one of the pivotal steps in the preliminary investigation. After analyzing all available information, consider the option to bring witnesses in to review a photo lineup to assist in identification, keeping in mind that if there was a chaotic scene, officer identification may be difficult. If naming the involved officer continues to be a problem, investigative office management staff should be consulted to determine how to proceed. For example, it could be advisable to continue with the investigation even if a specific officer is not identified when there is an issue of whether the incident was supervised appropriately per agency policy.

Where the alleged misconduct involves a single officer who cannot be identified despite all efforts to do so, and no other allegations about the incident are raised, it may be appropriate to suspend or close the investigation. However, even in these situations, there are potential policy or training recommendations that could emerge and be moved forward.

CONDUCTING AN OFFICER PHOTO LINEUP

When it is difficult to identify the involved officer a photo lineup can be used. Considerable research has established that the method used for conducting a photo lineup can impact its outcome. The investigative office must keep current with research and legal standards for conducting photo arrays. Examples of important considerations include:

- Choosing officers' photos that are similar in appearance to one another, but not so similar as to make identification confusing.
- Selecting the number of photos to use in the lineup.
- Determining whether photos are to be shown one at a time or displayed simultaneously.
- Informing the complainant that the subject officer may or may not be in the group of photos displayed.

To support the potential need for use in identifying officers, whether for law enforcement or misconduct investigation purposes, it is important that the law enforcement agency maintain photos of officers. Photos should be:

- Updated routinely.
- Available for all officers in both uniform and plainclothes, with and without a hat.
- Representative of the officer's current appearance considering facial hair, hair color, tattoos, and any other distinguishing characteristics.

The investigator should document the photos presented and the method of conducting the photo spread in the case file.

5. *Developing an Investigative Plan*

As soon as possible after completing the intake interview, the investigator should begin developing an Investigative Plan (IP) to focus and guide the investigation. This is the time when the interview is freshest in the investigator's memory, which will help in identifying witnesses, listing documents and physical evidence to collect, setting priorities for the preliminary investigation, and determining other investigative steps to be taken. Depending on the seriousness of the allegations and the likelihood that the complaint will proceed to a full investigation, the IP may be relatively informal or involve more specific requirements, as discussed in Chapter 3.B. The IP should be reviewed and updated as the complaint is assessed and the investigation proceeds, both by the investigator and supervisory staff.

6. *Conducting the Preliminary Investigation*

Preliminary investigations involve the collection of basic evidence, in addition to the complainant's intake statement, to enable an initial assessment of the complaint. Preliminary investigations should be handled as quickly as is reasonable under the circumstances, since evidence related to an incident can be lost or destroyed and witnesses' memories may fade with time.

A more detailed discussion about identifying and gathering evidence during the investigation is provided in Chapter 3.B. However, some preliminary steps should be taken during the intake and assessment phase. The complainant and others familiar with the police event should be asked about the existence of any photographs, video, or other recordings of the incident, and how copies can be obtained. Consideration should be given to whether an immediate site visit should be conducted to take photographs and search for witnesses, video/audio recordings, or other information that could help document what occurred before evidence becomes unobtainable. Perishable evidence should be requested or subpoenaed as early as possible.

All law enforcement department documentation related to the incident should be obtained; e.g., police reports, dispatch records, citations, departmental video/audio recordings, and other reports and documents routinely generated during a police incident. Police policies typically include specific reporting requirements for use of force incidents. If misuse of force is alleged, request all incident and use of force reports during the preliminary investigation.

If it is determined that using traditional news outlets, social media, canvassing or other approaches to reach the public is necessary to identify witnesses or evidence, this may need to be initiated during the intake/preliminary investigation process.

7. *Preliminary Steps for Investigating Allegations of Bodily Injury*

If there is an allegation regarding use of force or claim of bodily harm resulting from a police incident, ask during the intake interview that the complainant describe any injury, and document the presence or absence of such injury as early as possible. Photograph or video any physical signs of an injury or lack thereof. Have the complainant sign a medical release allowing the investigative office to collect medical records and follow up with all medical personnel who treated the complainant after the police incident, such as first responders, paramedics or emergency medical technicians (EMT's), hospital emergency room staff, and personal physicians. Medical records should be requested as soon as feasible, as obtaining such documents takes time and can create delays.

OFF-DUTY CONDUCT

Jurisdictions differ as to whether complaints related to an officer's off-duty conduct can be administratively investigated. Generally, there must be a nexus between the off-duty misconduct and the officer's law enforcement job in order for an administrative investigation to take place.

If the officer engages in activity off-duty that might be deemed criminal, the nexus is more easily established, while other off-duty conduct may not be as closely linked to police work. The investigative office should carefully consider whether it has jurisdiction to handle a particular complaint of off-duty misconduct, which might be categorized as "conduct unbecoming an officer."

A law enforcement agency's mission statement, code of ethics, and oath of office should provide clear guidelines on the organization's expectations for both on- and off-duty conduct, and highlight how officer conduct can positively or negatively affect the public's trust in the police agency.

C. Defining Allegations and Assessing the Underlying Incident for Additional Claims

After initial information is gathered about the complainant's concerns through the intake interview and preliminary investigation, specific allegations must be identified by consulting the law enforcement department's policy manual and other agency sources delineating officer conduct expectations.

A complaint can involve one or more allegations of misconduct against a single officer or multiple officers. Generally, all misconduct allegations stemming from the same underlying police incident will be grouped into one complaint, regardless of the number of officers involved.

In cases in which evidence of misconduct is uncovered later in an investigation, particularly if implicating officers who previously had not been named, consideration should be given to creating  a separate complaint. This might be advisable to ensure notice and other procedural requirements are met, and to avoid unnecessarily complicating the original complaint or risk missing investigation completion deadlines.

Allegation types and the specific terminology used will vary between law enforcement jurisdictions, as will authority to investigate certain types of complaints. Though this is not an exhaustive list of all allegations, typical claims raised in complaints and the variety of terminology used to describe police misconduct include:

- Abuse of discretion, unwarranted action
- Biased policing, discrimination, racial profiling
- Conduct unbecoming an officer, conduct reflecting discredit on the department
- Discourteous behavior, rudeness, unprofessional attitude
- Dishonesty
- Excessive force, unnecessary use of force, misuse of force
- Failure to comply or follow procedures
- Failure to follow video/audio recording requirements
- Failure to meet training or other qualification expectations
- Failure to report misconduct of another officer

- Failure to supervise
- Harassment
- Improper stop, search, seizure, or arrest
- Neglect of duty or failure to respond, adequately investigate, complete reports, or provide quality service
- Retaliation
- Violation of criminal law

Again, conduct expectations for law enforcement officers are initially set by federal and state law and are delineated by the law enforcement agency's policies; allegations of misconduct should be tied to the specific requirements detailed in the agency's policy manual. However, because it is impossible to regulate every unique problem that may arise, a broad category such as "conduct unbecoming an officer" is used to cover incidents that do not fall within a particular allegation type, but nonetheless reflect poorly on the officer and the law enforcement agency.

Determining the allegations to be investigated is a crucial element of the intake process. The complaint narrative should be carefully scrutinized to ensure that all issues raised are addressed. While the complainant should be asked about the concerns they want investigated, it is important to assess the complainant's statement and surrounding facts to define the appropriate allegations to pursue. The complainant may also raise issues about a policy or practice that they feel is improper that may not involve allegations against a specific officer. These types of concerns should be logged and flagged for review as the investigation proceeds. A specific conduct issue raised in a complaint that has not been addressed previously by an agency's policy manual could also lead to a recommendation to create a policy on point at the conclusion of the investigation.

It is also important at this stage to determine if there are additional allegations to investigate beyond those raised by the complainant. There may be departmental guidelines that appear to have not been followed during the incident in question, and an allegation of failure to comply or follow procedures should be incorporated into the investigation. Examples of issues that could be outside of the complainant's awareness, but may need to be investigated, include failure to: follow use of force reporting requirements, adhere to pursuit guidelines, complete incident reports, properly investigate an incident, or properly supervise.

D. Investigative Timelines, Communicating with Complainants and Officers, and Complaint Tracking

Maintaining investigative integrity requires that evidence be properly collected and secured when it is available and that interviews are conducted when witnesses' recollections are freshest. All parties to the complaint process should be informed of investigation timelines and updated if there are significant delays. Databases should be utilized to track investigations and provide alerts as timeline milestones approach.

Some states have enacted legislation that requires that the officer named in a misconduct complaint receive detailed information about the complaint, limits the amount of time a complainant has to file allegations of misconduct, limits the time during which an officer can be investigated and disciplined, and regulates who can question an officer, where an interview must take place, and under what conditions.[1] Even where such legislation does not exist, the complaint investigation process often is regulated through law enforcement agency policy, a collective bargaining contract, or other mechanism. Investigative offices should develop a list of specific procedural requirements in their jurisdiction to ensure consistent compliance.

1. Investigative Timelines

Resolution of complaints in a timely manner provides assurance to complainants and the community that concerns are taken seriously. An effective system requires that officers are exonerated as quickly as possible when not responsible for alleged misconduct, while those who require corrective action are disciplined swiftly to correct unacceptable behavior.

Investigative agencies must develop investigation timelines based upon the legal or contractual mandates in their jurisdictions, and set parameters for any timeline extensions to ensure investigation integrity. While some complaints can be investigated relatively quickly, others are more complicated and require numerous interviews, the collection of records and other evidence from outside sources, or expert analysis, all of which can be very time consuming. Each investigative agency must prioritize its caseload and set timeline goals in light of staff resources available, while bearing in mind that the review and discipline process following the investigation also takes time and legal and contractual limits must be observed.

2. Communicating with Complainants and Officers

Notice should be provided to the complainant acknowledging receipt of the complaint and explaining the complaint handling process. The precise notice to be given to subject officers may be dictated by statute, law enforcement agency policy, or a collective bargaining agreement. Notice to the parties should be timely, reference a case number, provide the investigator's name and contact information, and summarize expected next steps and timelines for the investigation. If the matter is resolved during the preliminary investigation or will be referred out, explain the reasoning behind the decision.

If the complaint will be further investigated, typically the complainant and named officer should receive regular updates. Some investigations can be quite lengthy and it is reassuring for the parties to be informed of the case status.

3. Tracking Systems

Systems have been developed that enable electronic tracking of complaints, personnel records, use of force, claims and litigation, and a myriad of other factors important to evaluating police conduct. In smaller departments, a spreadsheet may suffice for such record keeping. For more information on topics useful to include in a tracking system, see Chapter 6.B.

Regardless of the case tracking system in use, basic information about the complaint should be entered upon receipt. Timely data entry ensures that complaints are not duplicated and that all parties are advised of the complaint. Database tracking of complaints provides investigators and supervisors an indication of whether the investigation is appropriately moving forward.

Where more than one organization is involved with processing misconduct complaints, shared complaint databases are very beneficial, allowing everyone concerned to review and track complaint-related information in real time, from intake through the investigation, determination, and discipline stages.

E. Mediation/Alternative Dispute Resolution Options

Some complaints, particularly those involving potential miscommunication or misperceptions between the complainant and an officer, may be suitable for mediation or other dispute resolution programs. Mediation is an alternative to the adversarial process and traditional means of handling complaints, and has been used successfully in many jurisdictions.

Mediation can benefit both the complainant and the officer by providing a means for them to meet in a neutral setting to work to understand the incident from each other's point of view. It is a valuable tool for less serious complaints or those in which the lack of evidence or witnesses might make it difficult to arrive at a definitive finding. Mediation also can offer a faster resolution of the complaint.[2]

MEDIATION CONSIDERATIONS

Mediation can be a preferred and timely method for resolution in certain cases, though it requires participants to be fully engaged in the process. Factors to consider in setting up a program include:

- Who provides the mediation service, what are the costs involved, and who is responsible for the costs? Is it possible to develop a pro-bono mediation service?
- Is participation voluntary or mandatory on the part of either the complainant or officer?
- What is the impact of mediation on the underlying complaint? Will the complaint be dismissed if mediation is successful? How is success determined? If the complainant does not appear for the mediation, is the complaint dismissed?
- Whether the complaint is successfully mediated or dismissed for reasons related to mediation, are the original allegations tracked for reoccurring complaints against the officer?

Protocols should be developed for mediation or similar programs. Alternative processes typically utilize mediators who are not affiliated with the involved officer's department or any associated investigative organization. Sample procedures and forms can be requested from departments with established mediation programs.

A variety of other approaches to resolving individual and community complaints with law enforcement have been developed. For example, restorative justice principles originally created to address the harm caused by criminal offenders to their victims have been extended to police–community relations through the use of Restorative Circles.[3]

Review Questions

1. What are some reasons the complainant should provide an uninterrupted statement concerning their complaint, before the investigator asks many questions to elicit more detail?
2. What is the difference between a preliminary and a full investigation?

3. Why might retaliation for filing a complaint of officer misconduct be of particular concern for a complainant who is an undocumented immigrant or homeless?
4. What are some reasons supporting a system of tracking complaints, from intake through the investigation, determination, and discipline (if any)?

Notes

1 As with all public employees, law enforcement employees have due process rights under the U.S. Constitution. In addition, some states have enacted statutes in various forms providing specific protections related to the investigation and disciplinary process involving public safety employees. Generally referred to as the Law Enforcement Officer Bill of Rights (LEOBOR), a statement of procedural due process rights has been adopted in various forms in California, Maryland, Illinois, Nevada, Wisconsin, and other states. See, for example, 2017 (9) AELE Mo.L.J.201 Employment Law Section—September 2017 and 2017; (10) AELE Mo.L.J.201 Employment Law Section—October 2017.

2 For more information about the benefits of mediation, see Barbara Attard, *In Praise of Mediation* (1999), accountabilityassociates.org/publications; and Howard P. Greenwald and Charlie Beck, "Bringing Sides Together: Community-Based Complaint Mediation," *The Police Chief* 85 (August 2018): 36–42.

3 See, for example, Andrea Brenneke, "A Restorative Circle in the Wake of a Police Shooting," *Tikkun Magazine* 27(1) (2012).

In Chapter 3

Complaint Classification and the Investigation Process

Chapter 3

Complaint Classification and the Investigation Process

After intake and the preliminary investigation are completed, and allegations have been delineated, the complaint should be classified according to how it will be handled. Given limited resources and competing demands, most investigative offices have procedures in place to determine which complaints should be given priority for investigation purposes. For example, complaints alleging misuse of force or racial bias may automatically be classified for investigation, while allegations of isolated, low-level discourteous behavior could be processed differently. Some options for resolving complaints involving less serious concerns include referring the case to the subject officer's supervisor for handling, resolving the complaint through a simplified investigation process by using written questions rather than interviews, or classifying the case for mediation.

Factors to be considered in the classification process include: (1) whether the complaint is related to another complaint or litigation; (2) whether the involved officer has received other similar misconduct allegations; and (3) whether the case should be referred out for a criminal investigation. Procedures should be developed to determine how complaints are classified, who makes the classification decision, and how the classification can be changed if evidence is discovered indicating the classification should be re-evaluated.

REFERRAL OF MINOR COMPLAINTS TO POLICE SUPERVISORS

If there is a system to refer less serious complaints to the subject officer's supervisor to handle, it is important that clear instructions are provided, time limits set, and procedures are in place for reporting back to the investigative office once the matter is concluded.

At a minimum, the supervisor handling the complaint should contact the complainant and subject officer to probe the issues raised. All steps taken should be documented, including any counseling or retraining of the officer that takes place.

Reporting back to the investigative office allows for quality review of the process, provides data to track the types of issues encountered in different parts of the organization, and documents the incident in the named officer's record.

A. Complaints Classified for Investigation

Most complaints will require additional investigative steps beyond interviewing the complainant and the preliminary investigation completed during the intake stage, whether handled by the investigative office or the named officer's chain of command. An evaluation of the case should be conducted after the preliminary investigation and initial interviews to determine the seriousness of the issues involved and case assignment priorities. See the textbox "Complaints That May Require Prioritization" in Chapter 2 for additional information. There should be a clear understanding of all timelines associated with the case. Law enforcement agencies that have concurrent jurisdiction with outside investigative offices should coordinate to ensure that investigation and discipline timelines are met and all available evidence is shared.

INVESTIGATIVE SUPERVISION

All investigative offices must develop standards requiring regular and ongoing supervision of investigations. Systematic supervision ensures that cases are handled in a timely manner, investigated thoroughly and consistent with agency standards, and any unusual issues are addressed.

Supervisory reviews should occur:

- Post-intake for purposes of quality control and case assignment.
- At regular intervals during the investigation to provide analytical support and ensure steady progress.
- During the final stage of the investigation to evaluate the thoroughness of the investigation and recommendations or findings, as discussed in Chapter 4.F.

B. Organizational Tools: Investigation Plan and Witness/Evidence Matrix

An Investigation Plan (IP) should be developed at this point, or updated if one was developed during intake. Development of the IP requires an in-depth analysis of the issues raised by the complainant in light of the law enforcement agency's expectations about officer conduct. The IP should clarify which issues are being investigated, provide an investigative strategy, identify potential witnesses or sources of information, set out timelines for conducting the investigation, and anticipate problems or suggest areas for further work.

It can be helpful in more complex cases to create a witness/evidence matrix as the investigation develops. The matrix charts relevant aspects of witnesses' statements and evidence, allowing the investigator to visually compare witnesses' responses and different sources of evidence, in the context of the allegations. The matrix can be incorporated into the IP, or be a separate document if the case is large and involves many witnesses.

1. Allegation Review

The IP should identify the specific violations of policy alleged against each named officer, and determine the elements that need to be established to prove or disprove each allegation. As discussed in Chapter 2.C., determining the allegations to be investigated is key to conducting a focused investigation and thorough review of the issues. Reviewing the department's policy manual and other directives concerning officer conduct enables investigators to correctly identify appropriate allegations, regardless of whether the complainant raised specific issues or they were flagged by the investigative office. The totality of the facts should be assessed to ensure that the officer(s) named and allegation(s) listed cover all the potential misconduct issues involved in the incident underlying the complaint. Copies of relevant law enforcement agency policies should be included in the case file.

2. *Identifying Individuals to Interview*

Outline in the IP all individuals to be interviewed, including the complainant, named officer(s), all other potential witnesses to the incident, others with relevant information whether present during the incident or not, and any subject matter experts. While the complainant is typically interviewed during the intake process, determine whether to conduct a follow-up interview, particularly if the original interview was not done in person. A second interview also may address issues and questions that have arisen in the interim, or help answer credibility concerns. Reviewing the transcript or notes of the intake interview will help make this decision.

Determine if there are other potential witnesses. There are many ways to locate witnesses (or identify potentially relevant evidence), including canvassing neighborhoods where and at the time of day the police incident happened, reaching out to community groups that may be familiar with issues raised in the complaint, and using social media.

Develop the order of witness interviews and identify any special considerations, such as whether anyone may be unavailable for a period, whether there is concern a witness would be less willing to participate as time passes, or whether a witness may provide information that would be helpful in interviewing others.

Police agency policy or other rules usually require officers to respond to an internal notice to appear for an interview. Also, investigative offices in some jurisdictions may have subpoena power or other authority to ensure cooperation by law enforcement witnesses. Similarly, some departments may utilize subpoena authority to require civilian witnesses to provide statements, while many agencies must depend on voluntary cooperation. Create an interview schedule bearing in mind potential difficulties in arranging for individuals to provide a statement and the time necessary to serve a subpoena or other notice prior to the interview date.

If either a law enforcement or civilian witness is expected to be reluctant or hostile, develop a strategy for conducting the interview. For example, it may be beneficial to conduct the interview of an uncooperative witness after other interviews have been completed, in order to frame questions based on knowledge gained from prior interviews.

WITNESS/EVIDENCE MATRIX

A matrix that lists and cross-references all witnesses and primary evidence is a helpful tool. The matrix provides a visual chart:

- Outlining issues to be explored with each witness.
- Detailing the physical scene and any special elements that should be reviewed with witnesses, to include vantage point, lighting, etc.
- Noting the relationship of witnesses to each other, the complainant, or the named officer(s).
- Noting key evidentiary statements from each witness.
- Highlighting discrepancies in a witness' statement, between witnesses, or with documentary or physical evidence.

3. *Identifying and Collecting Documentary/Physical Evidence*

Identifying and collecting documents and physical evidence should begin during the intake process. As the IP is developed, an inventory of items collected and those still needed should be recorded and regularly updated to keep the file current with complete information. The lists in this section are guides to the types of documents and physical evidence that are important to collect in misconduct investigations. Each investigative office should create a checklist of typical documentary and physical evidence that is used by the law enforcement agency, using specific terminology common to that jurisdiction to ensure consistency and thoroughness of investigations. Issuing a subpoena or making a request for materials early in the investigative process will bring evidence in more expeditiously and provide notice to preserve perishable evidence, such as video/audio that could be recorded over or destroyed.

Types of Evidence Potentially Relevant in Police Misconduct Complaints

EXAMPLES OF DOCUMENTS

- Arrestee booking forms
- Death records, including coroner's report, inquest and grand jury records
- Detention or field identification forms required to document a detention or questioning in the field
- Dispatch and call records
- Fire department/medic/ambulance communication records or reports
- Incident reports, statements, and other records associated with the incident underlying the complaint
- Jail or youth detention records
- Medical records and signed consent for release regarding any injuries to an involved party, including emergency treatment, hospital records, and follow-up care
- Motor vehicle or licensing records
- Notes, diagrams, email, memoranda, correspondence
- Parking or traffic citations
- Payroll or other personnel records
- Policies, operational or unit manuals or directives
- Precinct, station, or duty rosters and assignments
- Property or evidence reports, including chain of custody records
- Prosecution filing or decline decisions
- Protection orders
- Search warrants, consent to search forms, or other evidence of consent
- Secondary employment permits
- Training protocols and records
- Use of force reports and associated documentation, including force review records

EXAMPLES OF PHYSICAL/ELECTRONIC EVIDENCE

- Cell phone texts, photos, and call records
- Communications recordings
- Department issued cell phone
- Electronic control weapon (ECW) downloads
- Photographs; e.g., booking photos, photos documenting use of force injuries, and photos of the scene

- Video/audio recordings: external; e.g., recordings from public cameras, business or private security systems, and witnesses' cell phones
- Video/audio recordings: internal; e.g., recordings from body cameras, in-car digital cameras, holding cells, officers' department issued cell phones, and surveillance cameras

OTHER INFORMATION SOURCES TO CONSIDER

Examples of other sources of information that could provide evidentiary leads or aid the investigation include:

- Broadcast news and outtake videos
- Laws and legal decisions related to the police action underlying the complaint
- Print or electronic news articles or blogs
- Social media postings

SUBJECT MATTER EXPERTS

As the investigation develops, determine if outside professional resources are needed to evaluate, review, store, or enhance the evidence. For example:

- It could be important to have a medical professional examine medical or autopsy records to clarify technical terms or ambiguities in the record or the impact of a medical condition on the issues in the complaint.
- A technical expert may be necessary if there is a need to enhance the quality of an video/audio recording to more clearly assess its relevance, or to verify the accuracy of a recording.
- It may be advisable to bring in an evidence specialist to examine weapons used in an incident and better understand the use of force issues involved.

In large departments the subject matter expert may be available within the law enforcement agency (provided objectivity can be assured), though all investigative offices should seek out external resources as needed.

4. Milestones and Timelines

The IP should set out a chronology for the investigation. It should identify all evidence that has been and still must be collected before witness interviews are conducted. The IP also should indicate the anticipated order of interviews, including any reason to conduct them in a special sequence.

Highlight in the IP whether the complaint is related to another complaint, an investigation by an outside agency, or litigation. If so, it may be important to coordinate the investigation or consider the timelines of all investigations.

Make an objective estimate as to how long each step of the investigation will take and whether there could be any problem in meeting the investigation deadline, with consideration of holidays, training schedules, workload, or scheduled absences (for the investigator and witnesses) that may impact the investigation timeline.

Set a deadline to complete the investigation, keeping in mind the various stages involved, including conducting the investigation, preparing the case report/summary, final organization of the case file after the investigation is completed, and the review and decision making process to determine the ultimate finding. Set specific milestones for all steps in the process, allowing for possible delays or the need for further investigation, while meeting the goal to complete the entire investigation in an expeditious manner, and within any mandated deadlines.

C. Witness Interview Strategies and Techniques

Well-conducted interviews can elicit reliable information, provide the investigator with new leads, and establish pivotal facts to resolve allegations. Interviews in police misconduct investigations sometimes can be difficult because they may be emotionally charged or technically complicated. Thoughtful and thorough preparation will ensure that the interview yields the best results possible.

1. Determining the Order and Timing of Interviews

Interviews should be scheduled in a manner allowing for interview preparation and notice to the witness. All efforts to contact a witness about scheduling an interview should be noted in the file. Generally, interviews should be conducted in the following order:

- Complainant
- Non-police witnesses
- Resource persons who may offer pivotal interpretive information that may assist in preparing questions for officer interviews
- Law enforcement department employee witnesses
- Named officer(s)[1]

With any given case, however, there can be a rationale for changing this order. For example, the named officer might be interviewed earlier, after the complainant and key witnesses, to determine what is conceded or contested, thus determining the need to track down and interview other witnesses. As mentioned above, witnesses expected to be uncooperative are sometimes best interviewed last, allowing the investigator to gather evidence from other sources and develop more focused questions, rather than relying on the witness to volunteer information. Witness interviews should be conducted in person unless there is a specific reason that is not possible, in which case the reason should be noted in the case log.

2. Interview Preparation Considerations—Documents and Topics to Cover

When preparing for an interview, it is important to review the IP to determine the issues to be addressed with the witness. Applicable laws and department policies/orders should be reviewed to ensure that questions cover all pertinent issues, to prove or disprove the complaint allegations. Determine if there are documents, video/audio, photos, or other evidence to present to and explore with the witness.

An outline of topics and subtopics to be covered with the witness should be prepared.[2] If specific questions are listed, open-ended phrasing should be used. Bear in mind that interview leads might be missed if the investigator over-relies on predetermined questions rather than focusing on the witness' responses.

3. *Conducting Investigations or Interviews with a Primary and Secondary Investigator*

It can be useful to assign two investigators to a single investigation or an interview, particularly if the case is complex, there are short deadlines, the investigators have related cases, or it is anticipated that a witness will be difficult to interview. In such cases, a second investigator can help enable a division of labor for completing investigative tasks and analyzing evidence.

Examples of cases that could benefit from assigning more than one investigator include questionable officer-involved shootings and complaints related to large demonstrations, which could involve multiple complainants, officers, and/or jurisdictions.

In an interview situation, the primary investigator on the case should take the lead, dictating strategy prior to the interview, controlling the flow of the interview, asking most of the questions, taking brief notes, and recording the interview. The secondary investigator can take thorough notes, identify areas where more probing is needed, and follow up with or suggest questions after the primary investigator is finished. Even if follow-up questions are unnecessary, the secondary investigator can share interview notes and observations about the witness' demeanor and other nonverbal behavior, which can be useful in assessing the overall testimony provided. Some jurisdictions limit the number of interviewers allowed to question an officer.

4. *Administrative and Legal Issues Specific to Interviewing Law Enforcement Witnesses*

Interviews of law enforcement personnel may be regulated by state statute, agency policy, and/or collective bargaining agreements that include set timelines and other requirements that must be built into the IP and interview schedule. Investigative offices should develop a list of procedural requirements in their specific jurisdiction to ensure consistent compliance.

a) Officer Interview Notifications

Interview notifications or subpoenas for law enforcement personnel that conform to legal, policy, and collective bargaining agreement requirements must be established. Generally, notice should be provided by departmental mail or email and include an order to appear, the date, time, and place of the interview, the name of the investigator conducting the interview, information about representation rights and consequences of failure to appear, a confidentiality directive, interview recording and transcription options, and, if required, a copy of the complaint allegations. An entry should be made in the case file that notice was sent to the employee (copied to the chain of command and union, if required or advisable), with a copy to the file, providing evidence of the date and time the interview notice was sent. Officer interviews will generally be conducted at the investigative office, though circumstances could require changing the location, date, or time to accommodate conflicts.

b) Interview Procedures—Officers' Rights

It is important to be aware that the officer named in the complaint and witness officers may have different rights in the interview process, depending on the issues involved. If criminal charges against the named officer might result from the incident, it is necessary to give the officer a *Garrity* advisement at the time of the interview, which serves to protect the officer's Fifth Amendment right against self-incrimination while allowing an administrative investigation to proceed. *Garrity v. New Jersey*, 385 U.S. 493 (1967). A *Garrity* advisement serves to acknowledge that the reason for the interview is administrative, and not for the purpose of furthering a criminal investigation or prosecution, that if any self-incriminating statements are made they cannot be used in a criminal proceeding, and that the officer is ordered to answer questions and could be terminated for refusing to do so. Investigative agencies should consult with legal counsel in developing a standard *Garrity* advisement to use when appropriate. See discussion in Chapter 7.C.3.

Witness officers generally do not have the same Fifth Amendment concerns or rights as officers named in a misconduct complaint with potential criminal implications. However, if a witness officer incriminates themself during an interview, steps must be taken to amend the complaint to name the officer who now may be subject to criminal charges, and to address the officer's rights before questioning continues. If permitted under the law of the jurisdiction, police agency policy, and the collective bargaining contract, the interview can continue after the witness is provided notice that they are now a subject of the complaint and is given a *Garrity* advisement (and allowed representation). However, many jurisdictions will require the interview to be stopped and a written notice issued, stating that the officer is being named in a complaint involving possible criminal matters. In such cases, the officer should be rescheduled for an interview as a named officer and provided a *Garrity* advisement when the questioning resumes.

If a witness officer testifies to possible misconduct that does not raise criminal issues, a decision will still have to be made about amending the complaint to name the witness officer with an added allegation. As with newly discovered evidence of criminal misconduct by a witness officer, notice of the amended complaint should be provided, with an opportunity to consult a representative. Depending on jurisdictional requirements and the officer's preference, the interview could continue following such notice and opportunity to involve a representative, or be rescheduled for a later date.

The approach to be followed by all investigators should be spelled out in office protocols so there is no question as to how to proceed if an officer offers self-incriminating testimony. If a question arises, a supervisor should be consulted about any ambiguities concerning procedural rules that apply with regard to providing notice, continuing or rescheduling the interview, and the officer's right to representation.

5. Interviewing Non-Law Enforcement Witnesses

For complainants and witnesses not employed by the law enforcement agency, interviews should be scheduled at the interviewee's convenience, while avoiding unnecessary delay in the investigation. Interviews with civilian witnesses should be confirmed with a written notice by mail or email including the date, time, and location of the interview. If a witness is difficult to locate or not returning phone calls, pursue other strategies to contact the individual.

When a witness' whereabouts are unknown, use due diligence to search for an address or phone number by checking records such as voter registration rolls, Department of Motor Vehicles records, and on-line research or commercial database companies, which can provide information derived from credit reports and other sources to identify a person's phone number, address, relatives, neighbors, and past residences and workplaces. If a witness' address is known, but they are not responding, consider a visit to establish contact. As a final step, a letter and/or email should be sent asking for the witness to contact the investigator, indicating a deadline by which the witness must respond in order to participate in the investigation. Note all efforts to reach the individual in the case file.

Civilian witnesses should be encouraged to be interviewed at the investigative office, although special considerations may necessitate holding the interview elsewhere (e.g., a witness is in jail or has no means of transport to come for an in-office interview). Witnesses (including the complainant) may need to take time away from their family or work to be interviewed, and finding ways to make the process more convenient may facilitate their participation. Also, interviewing a witness in familiar surroundings may contribute to a more relaxed and complete interview.

Interviewing the complainant or a witness at the site of the incident may be beneficial if being on location is important for better understanding details about the incident. If it is necessary to conduct civilian witness interviews in the field, supervisors should be consulted and consideration given to having a second investigator attend for safety reasons.

6. Recording the Interview

All interviews, whether in-person or by telephone, should be recorded in their entirety, as a safeguard to ensure there is a precise record. Law enforcement employees may be obligated to submit to recorded interviews, although consent to the recording should be noted at the beginning of the interview. Witnesses who are not law enforcement personnel should be told the rationale for recording interviews and encouraged to consent, with consent noted on the record.

As discussed in the context of the intake interview in Chapter 2, if consent is not provided, or the interview is not recorded for some other reason, document the refusal or rationale for not recording and prepare a narrative summary of the interview immediately afterward. When feasible, ask the witness to review the summary, note any changes needed, and sign the document. The recording and transcript or the interview summary should be placed in the file; a duplicate copy should be provided to the witness upon request. A collective bargaining contract or department policy may require that a copy of an audio recording or transcript of the interview be routinely provided to officers and complainants. Interviewees occasionally bring their own device to record the interview, which should be permitted.

HANDLING CONFLICT OF INTEREST SITUATIONS

As discussed in Chapter 8.D., it is important that investigative offices institute policies to prevent investigators being involved in real or perceived conflict of interest situations. A policy should be developed mandating that investigators report any conflict and another investigator should be assigned. This may be difficult in small departments and require the investigative office to turn to outside resources. Note that merely having worked with or being familiar with an involved party should not automatically create a conflict. Any such concerns should be discussed with a supervisor.

7. Setting the Tone and Introductory Remarks

The investigator's demeanor during the interview should be respectful, courteous, and professional. It is very important to maintain formality and neutrality, even if the interviewee is someone known to the investigator. Each person interviewed should be addressed by their surname. If it will be difficult to maintain neutrality with a witness for any reason, the issue should be raised with a supervisor as soon as a conflict is recognized and someone else should conduct the interview.

An introductory script to be used in all interviews should be developed. The script should guide the investigator in identifying each person present in the interview room, as well as provide: the case number; complainant's name; the name of the witness; the date, time, and location of the interview; an acknowledgement by the witness that notice was received; and the *Garrity* advisement (if applicable). The script should be filled out in advance and read aloud at the start of the interview, to ensure this information is on the record. Next, the investigator should provide a brief explanation about the purpose of the interview; e.g., "The purpose of this interview is to discuss a complaint filed by Mr. Dave Johnson, case #XX, regarding an incident that happened on January 15, 2020, at the intersection of Market and Vine."

8. Asking Proper Questions to Elicit Authentic and Complete Statements

Once preliminary matters are completed, use an open-ended question to ask the witness to describe the incident underlying the complaint, such as, "Please would you tell me what happened on January 15, 2020, when you had an encounter with the police?" or "Would you please describe what took place when you observed Mr. Johnson interacting with police officers on January 15, 2020?" Allow the witness to provide an uninterrupted narrative of the incident, with encouragement as needed, "And then what happened?" or "Is there anything else about the incident you remember?" The interviewer should note follow-up questions to be asked at the end of the interviewee's narrative to avoid interruptions, if possible.

While helping the witness to stay on track, do not unnecessarily confine the person to discussing only the specific violations alleged against the named officer. Rather, encourage the witness to describe everything experienced during the event. This may lead to other witnesses or evidence, or information about actions by the named or other officers not described by the complainant, such as officers' comments when the complainant was not present.

After encouraging the witness to provide a full statement, follow-up interview questions should address the elements related to the specific policy violations at issue in the allegations against the named officer(s). Some witnesses may be able to speak to all elements of all allegations, while others may offer more limited information. While using an interview outline as a guide can be helpful to ensure coverage of all issues, it is important to maintain eye contact with the witness, listen closely to the answers provided to consider the need for follow-up questions or clarifications, and observe body language and other nonverbal communication. Again, investigators should be flexible and not stay so wedded to an outline that the opportunity to pursue an unexpected line of information is lost.

At times it may be necessary to challenge assertions and probe further, in a non-judgmental way, if there are incomplete responses or there is a discrepancy between the witness' statement and other testimony or evidence. If possible, investigators should anticipate how interviewees might respond to specific points of contention and prepare questions ahead of time to ensure follow-up, as needed.

Also, personal biases may influence the witness' perception. Sometimes biases are indicated by unexplained assumptions in a witness' statement, such as, "Cops have nothing better to do than harass people." or "Those kids didn't belong in that neighborhood, so I stopped them." Statements indicating possible bias should be probed further for clarification.

9. Leading versus Non-Leading Questions

Non-leading, open-ended questions should be used to elicit the witness' testimony. Investigators should allow the witness to fully respond without interruption so the witness offers as much detail as possible before the investigator follows up with additional questions. Leading questions that can be answered with a "yes" or "no," or questions with the answer implied, should be avoided. With leading questions, the investigator is, in effect, providing a rationale or explanation to the witness while asking the question. Avoid questions that assume facts not previously articulated by the witness or otherwise established, as these can suggest information the witness may unwittingly incorporate into their answer.

NON-LEADING VERSUS LEADING QUESTIONS

Use Open-Ended Questions	Avoid Leading Questions
What did you observe when you arrived?	Do you remember seeing the subject with a gun when you arrived?
Where were you when you saw the subject?	Were you next to your car when you saw the subject?
Who was present?	Were Officers Smith and Jones present?
What did Officer Smith say?	Did Officer Smith say that the subject had a weapon?
Why did you use your taser?	Did you use your taser because the subject would not drop his weapon after you asked him to?
What were you thinking as the incident unfolded?	You were worried about your safety, right?
What did the officers communicate to you?	Did the other officers ask for your assistance?

10. Establishing a Clear and Complete Record of the Interview

Developing a clear record of all the information a witness can offer is the primary objective of the interview. Interviews should move from broad to more specific questions. The use of repetition can be helpful to understand details by restating what was heard to ensure accuracy. It is important to avoid making extraneous comments or expressing judgment verbally or by tone of voice about the witness' statement.

Witnesses should be advised that they must answer all questions audibly. Any nodding, pointing, or other gestures should be verbally acknowledged on the record. For example, if the witness points to someone or something in the room, the investigator should specify what the witness indicated and ask the witness for confirmation.

Using tools to help understand what happened can clarify the interviewee's statement. For example, the investigator can present a document, map, diagram, photo, or video to assist the witness in detailing what happened, or the investigator can ask the witness to create a diagram or other drawing to help explain the testimony. Assuming the statement is being recorded, any descriptive tools used must be audibly noted and clearly explained. For example, if the witness watches an in-car video of an event and comments, note on the record the exact point in the video that the comment was made. Similarly, if the witness draws a diagram of the incident scene, describe the diagram for the record; for example, "The diagram drawn by Witness A has Mr. Johnson's car located at the top of the page, on a line he has labeled 1st Avenue, with the front of the car pointed toward the left side of the page, toward a line he has labeled Madison Street, indicating it was heading north. Does that correctly represent your drawing, Witness A?" Any such tool used with the witness should be labeled and included in the case file.

It is also important to establish the relationship between all parties present at the incident. Perceptions, statements, and credibility may vary depending on the interviewee's relationship to others. For example, witnesses who are friends or are married, or two officers who were at the scene, may have discussed the incident outside the interview, which could influence their testimony. Regardless of known relationships, all witnesses should be asked if they have discussed the case with anyone. If it appears that a witness' testimony has been influenced by another witness, it would be important to explore how the testimony may have been impacted by earlier discussions of the incident.

If conflicts in testimony or with evidence (videos, incident reports, photos, etc.) arise, it is best to clarify such issues in a forthright, direct manner, without expressing judgment. For example, "I'm confused because you said you returned to the precinct after the incident, but dispatch records indicate you immediately responded to another call. Please help me understand this."

If relevant, law enforcement witnesses should be asked about their understanding of the departmental policy at issue and any related training they have received. For example, with an allegation that the complainant was handcuffed unnecessarily during the incident, it would be appropriate to ask the officer whether there is a departmental policy concerning handcuffing, what the policy provides, the circumstances in which handcuffing is permitted, advised, or prohibited, and the training received concerning handcuffing protocols.

II. Concluding the Interview

Before ending the interview, ask if the witness has any other information about the incident or complaint that has not been addressed, including whether the witness is aware of other witnesses or evidence. This line of questioning is important to ask of all witnesses to ensure that information is not missed because an earlier question was not worded properly or an issue was inadvertently overlooked. For witnesses who are not law enforcement employees, it is useful to verify contact and back-up information in case there are follow-up questions.

When concluding a named officer interview, if the collective bargaining contract or a policy allows a union representative or attorney to be present for an officer's interview, there should be a clear protocol as to whether the officer's representative can ask questions of the officer once the investigator completes questioning. Some criticize the practice as unnecessarily providing the representative an opportunity to slant the record, and as an infringement on management rights. However, allowing questioning by the officer's representative may provide insight as to defenses the officer will raise as the case proceeds, and contributes to the officer's sense of fairness and legitimacy in the complaint investigation process.

D. Completing the Investigation—Reviewing the Investigation Plan

After using the IP to guide the investigation, it should be reviewed again at the point the investigation appears complete. It is not unusual to discover gaps or discrepancies in testimony between witnesses or with other evidence, as the final review of the IP is conducted and the investigator begins drafting the investigative report. Check to see that all relevant and available documents and other evidence have been collected and analyzed, and that all individuals with relevant information about the complaint have been identified in the IP and interviewed. Consider whether any final attempts should be made to reach witnesses who could not be located earlier.

Finally, be sure that all steps that have been taken during the investigation are documented in the IP, including those taken during the final review. Provide an explanation if potentially relevant documentary or physical evidence or witness testimony is missing.

Review Questions

1. When would it be important to assign a second investigator in a case?
2. Is it recommended to detail every question to be asked in an interview? Why might sticking to pre-scripted questions negatively impact the integrity of the investigation?
3. Describe the difference between leading and open-ended questions and provide examples. Which type of questions are recommended for fact-finding interviews, and why?
4. What is an Investigative Plan (IP) and how is it used? When should it be developed and updated?

Notes

1 For more information regarding the importance of planning the order of interviews, see Lou Reiter, *Law Enforcement Administrative Investigations* (Legal and Risk Management Institute, Public Agency Training Council, 2006), p. 5.6.

2 For sample interview outlines for subject/witness officers and complainant/civilian witnesses, see Jeffrey J. Noble and Geoffrey P. Alpert, *Managing Accountability Systems for Police Conduct: Internal Affairs and External Oversight* (Waveland Press, 2009), Appendix A and B.

In Chapter 4

Finalizing the Investigation

Evaluating Evidence, Determining Findings, Making Recommendations, Report Writing, and Complaint Closure

A. Standard of Review
B. Evaluating Evidence and Making Credibility Determinations
C. Investigation Findings
D. Summarizing the Evidence and Completing the Investigative Report
E. Recommendations Stemming from Issues Discovered During Complaint Investigations
F. Supervisory Review of Completed Investigations
G. Discipline and Other Corrective Action
H. Complaint Closure: File Organization Review, Notification to Parties, and Transmission of Case Records
I. Data Collection

Chapter 4

Finalizing the Investigation

Evaluating Evidence, Determining Findings, Making Recommendations, Report Writing, and Complaint Closure

Upon completion, the misconduct investigation must be evaluated to determine recommended findings. This process depends on having an organized case file to ensure a thorough and complete review of the investigation. Developing or updating a witness/evidence matrix outlining key statements and evidence can provide a visual analytical tool, and is particularly helpful in complex cases.

PREPONDERANCE OF THE EVIDENCE

Determinations in administrative law enforcement misconduct investigations are most commonly made according to the preponderance of the evidence standard. This standard has been described as meaning:

- More likely than not
- More than 50%
- A tipping of the scales of justice

The preponderance of the evidence standard is based on the more convincing evidence and its probable truth or accuracy, not on the amount of evidence available on one side or the other.

A. Standard of Review

Once an investigation is complete, a finding must be made with regard to each allegation raised in the complaint. In administrative investigations of complaints of police misconduct, the finding is typically made based on the "preponderance of the evidence" standard. Using this standard, a sustained finding means that it is more likely than not that the named officer engaged in the alleged misconduct. As a matter of law or pursuant to a collective bargaining contract, some jurisdictions use a "clear and convincing" standard of proof. This higher standard requires a showing that the alleged misconduct was highly probable. The "beyond a reasonable doubt" standard is reserved for weighing evidence in criminal proceedings to determine if the prosecution's case overcomes the presumption that a person is innocent until proven guilty.

If officers can appeal a finding of misconduct to arbitration under a collective bargaining contract or otherwise, disciplinary action likely would be reviewed for "just cause." Under principles of labor arbitration, an arbitrator typically considers both the evidence of misconduct and whether the proposed discipline is appropriate, possibly taking into account factors such as the officer's length of service and overall performance. While the preponderance of the evidence standard often is used during arbitration, a clear and convincing standard of proof might be applied instead, particularly if significant discipline such as termination is involved. Anticipating the possibility of appeal, at least where there is serious misconduct and heightened discipline, analyzing evidence under both the preponderance of the evidence and clear and convincing standards could increase the likelihood that the investigative findings and discipline will survive review.

B. Evaluating Evidence and Making Credibility Determinations

There will be conflicting evidence in some cases, which will require that credibility determinations be made. When conflicting testimony or other evidence is collected, investigators must consider whether someone is being dishonest or there is another explanation for the discrepancy. For example, a video recording can confirm the perspective of a particular witness' vantage point, while other witnesses might provide seemingly contradictory testimony based on their location relative to the incident. Video footage is limited by camera angle and scope, and may not necessarily capture all of the activity that is occurring or the events that led up to a police encounter. In some instances the sound and picture in video footage can be out of synch and misleading, and may require professional analysis. Conflicting testimony or other evidence must be assessed to determine whether the conflict can be reconciled or explained, or indicates a credibility issue with one or more of the witnesses. Reviewing (or developing) a witness matrix to compare statements and supporting or refuting evidence is particularly helpful in analyzing cases with apparent conflicts. See Chapter 3.B. for more information about use of a witness/evidence matrix.

The perceptions of the officer, complainant, and witnesses may also be impacted by a host of circumstances that can limit their ability to accurately perceive an incident. Such factors include fear for physical safety, lighting, proximity, and information shared by others during or after the event. Other factors that could impact a person's perceptions include their emotional state, fatigue (e.g., the end of the officer's shift or a witness' work day, or a witness awakened in the middle of the night), hearing or sight limitations, or the influence of medication, alcohol, or drugs. Interviews about an incident might take place weeks, months, or even years after an event, possibly making it more difficult for witnesses to accurately recall all details.

Any of these factors could contribute to a witness giving testimony at odds with their earlier statement or other testimony or evidence collected in the investigation. Different perspectives about an incident do not necessarily mean someone is being dishonest, although some differences may require that a credibility determination be made.

Issues to consider when weighing credibility include:

- Whether the testimony is inherently plausible.
- The witness' demeanor.
- Whether the witness makes a statement against self-interest, such as admitting to improper or illegal activity.
- Whether the witness has a motive to falsify.
- Whether the statement is consistent with the witness' previous testimony or other evidence.
- Whether significant time has passed since the incident that could impact the completeness and accuracy of the witness' testimony.
- Whether there is corroborating testimony or other evidence supporting the witness' testimony.

- The amount of detail in the witness' statement.
- Statements that indicate a possible bias.

Credibility determinations can be difficult to make, but when necessary, the investigator should thoroughly describe all factors supporting the evaluation of whether or not the witness is telling the truth. Directly questioning a witness about a discrepancy between their statement and other statements or evidence is pivotal in any credibility analysis.

Similarly, the investigator may need to assess the credibility of documents collected during an investigation. Whether a document is identified and collected by the investigator or offered by a law enforcement witness, the complainant, or another civilian witness, all documents should be reviewed for reliability and trustworthiness. The analysis should indicate how each relevant document supports or calls into question other evidence or witness statements.

The investigator should review all materials gathered during the investigation, resolve any outstanding credibility issues, and make a preliminary recommendation as to the finding, using the preponderance of the evidence standard. Review and discussion with supervisors should determine the need for further investigation or that the case is ready for final disposition.

C. Investigation Findings

While departments can use different labels or disposition categories for administrative investigations, a typical scheme (assuming the preponderance of the evidence standard) includes the following findings:

- **Sustained:** The allegation of misconduct is supported by a preponderance of the evidence.
- **Proper Conduct or Exonerated:** The preponderance of the evidence indicates the conduct underlying the complaint was justified and consistent with policy.
- **Not Sustained or Inconclusive:** The allegation of misconduct cannot be proved or disproved by a preponderance of the evidence.
- **Unfounded or Frivolous:** There are no facts in support of the misconduct allegation or the preponderance of the evidence indicates the incident, as alleged, did not occur.

D. Summarizing the Evidence and Completing the Investigative Report

Once all steps in the investigation have been completed, the evidence should be summarized. The matrix is a useful visual tool for reviewing evidence at this stage. In order to arrive at a finding, all evidence relevant to each allegation should be thoroughly analyzed in light of the applicable standard of proof and summarized in a written document.

One way to give structure to a complex set of facts and questions is to organize the investigative report following the Issue/Rule/Application/Conclusion (IRAC) methodology, which is often taught in law schools.

IRAC provides a systematized formula for analyzing evidence. Begin with a concise, but thorough summary of the relevant facts of the complaint. Then, using the preponderance of the evidence standard, detail the analysis for each allegation for each named officer separately:

- **Issue:** State the allegation.
- **Rule:** List the law enforcement agency policy, directive, or other rule governing conduct expectations that applies to the allegation.

- **Application:** Detail how the evidence collected in the investigation supports or negates the allegation at issue in light of department policy. Evaluate any conflicting facts or credibility issues.
- **Conclusion:** State the finding or recommended finding for the allegation in light of the analysis, based upon the preponderance of the evidence standard.[1]

Another approach to organizing and analyzing investigative evidence, which can be used in conjunction with IRAC, is to prepare an outline structured by issue, chronologically, or by named officer, with subheadings addressing the evidence and findings.[2] For example, the investigator might list all the allegations against one named officer, with the evidence that supports or disputes each allegation, and delineate proposed findings, before moving on to analyze the allegations against another officer.

Any analytic approach to summarizing the investigation may require that some evidence is repeated, as it will be relevant to more than one allegation or named officer. Whatever approach is used, the investigator must go beyond a superficial evaluation of the evidence to explicitly discuss the evidence, particularly where there are inconsistencies in testimony, witness credibility issues, or other complexities. Ultimately, the goal is to present the evidence in a manner that helps the ultimate decision maker sort through all the relevant information that has been collected to more efficiently arrive at a disposition.

E. Recommendations Stemming from Issues Discovered During Complaint Investigations

Regardless of the finding(s) in a complaint, the investigation may reveal policy or training issues to be evaluated. The investigative office should identify problem areas for review by the law enforcement agency and track any recommendations, findings, or issues for follow-up. For example, an officer might be exonerated on an allegation of mishandling evidence, though the investigation results in a recommendation that the department develop more robust evidence processing and storage procedures. Similarly, the investigation may reveal supervisory issues, staffing or equipment concerns, or other organizational problems that should be considered for further action. The investigative office could draft specific change recommendations or refer the findings to the unit involved with reviewing and developing changes in training or policy.

Referrals for policy or training review should be tracked to ensure that the policy or practice at issue is reviewed within a set period, with feedback to the investigative office upon completion or an explanation as to why the recommendation was not implemented. During the closure process, such issues should be flagged with an action plan for follow-up. Any recommendations arising from misconduct cases should be presented in routine reports about investigative office activity.

CHANGES RECOMMENDED ALTHOUGH ALLEGATIONS NOT PROVEN AGAINST OFFICER WHO SHOT MICHAEL BROWN JR.

In 2014, in Ferguson, Missouri, Michael Brown Jr., an 18-year-old African American man, was fatally shot by Darren Wilson, a 28-year-old white police officer. An investigation by the U.S. Department of Justice (DOJ) determined that there was insufficient evidence to prove that Officer Wilson's actions violated federal criminal civil rights laws. The DOJ determined that forensic and physical evidence and testimony from witnesses supported Officer

Wilson's account that he shot Brown in self-defense. Despite this outcome, a related DOJ investigation determined that the Ferguson Police Department (FPD) and Ferguson Municipal Court engaged in a pattern or practice of conduct violating the First, Fourth, and Fourteenth Amendments of the U.S. Constitution, disproportionately impacting the African American community. The investigation found constitutional violations that included: stops without reasonable suspicion, arrests without probable cause, interference with the right to freedom of expression, use of excessive force, and that the Municipal Court focused on revenue generation over public safety.

The DOJ and Ferguson subsequently entered into a Consent Decree to address these concerns. The agreement provides over 400 policy and training reforms for the FPD and Municipal Court to address the constitutional violations and includes a commitment to: hold public servants accountable for misconduct; develop a system that incorporates civilian input into all aspects of policing, including policy development, training, use of force review, and investigation of misconduct complaints; involve the Civilian Review Board to promote awareness of the misconduct complaint system; maintain a community-based mediation program as an alternative to resolve misconduct complaints, where appropriate; and adopt a cost-feasible data collection plan.[3]

F. Supervisory Review of Completed Investigations

Supervisors reviewing investigative files and case reports should evaluate investigation benchmarks including whether:

- All key witnesses were interviewed.
- Interviews were thorough.
- Relevant documentary and physical evidence was collected.
- Investigative procedures were followed.
- All evidence was fairly and properly evaluated.
- A determination can be made regarding each allegation raised in the complaint.
- Any policy or training recommendations are to be made.
- Investigation timelines were met.

If key information is missing, there should be a written explanation in the file of attempts made by the investigator to secure the evidence or stated reasons why it was not sought. Following discussion with the investigator, the supervisor should decide whether further investigation is necessary. If so, any additional steps should be completed as expeditiously as possible and the file and summary of the evidence amended, as needed.

G. Discipline and Other Corrective Action

Regardless of whether the investigative office, law enforcement executive, or other authority determines findings, if a complaint is sustained it is important that discipline be meted out in a fair and timely manner. A primary purpose of any system to address misconduct is to change unacceptable behavior. Depending on the circumstances of the case, an effective response to address misconduct could include counseling, training, unpaid time off, demotion, termination, or other outcomes.

Some jurisdictions offer alternative avenues to corrective action in sustained cases, such as giving officers the opportunity to engage in mediation or another dispute resolution process to remedy the concerns raised in the complaint. See Chapter 2.E. for more information. Another approach is "Education Based Discipline," in which officers are required to waive their discipline appeal rights in exchange for receiving training on decision making and conduct expectations, instead of unpaid time off.[4] This method has the advantage of resolving allegations more quickly, with potentially less financial impact for the subject employee and their family, and the opportunity to engage in adult based learning rather than traditional discipline.

Any disciplinary structure should ensure that discipline is progressive and appropriate in light of factors including: the law enforcement department's disciplinary structure, discipline imposed in comparable cases, the officer's past conduct history, the officer's training history and training needs, and the seriousness of the issues involved in the current case.

H. Complaint Closure: File Organization Review, Notification to Parties, and Transmission of Case Records

Once an investigation is complete, there are a number of steps that should be taken at the closure stage. At this point, all related case information should have been collected into a hard copy and/or digital file readily accessible for a variety of purposes, including discovery in any related criminal or civil litigation, personnel record reviews, or review or appeal by the complainant or subject officer, as allowed. Data entry also is an important step in the closure process to ensure that all fields of the complaint tracking system are updated, as discussed in the next section.

After final review, notice should be provided to the complainant and the subject officer that the investigation is complete and indicating the final disposition or finding. When there is no conflict with confidentiality rules, providing a summary of the evidence can enhance accountability and transparency of the process. If the investigation will undergo further review, or if either party has appeal rights, applicable procedures should be explained. Provide investigator contact information in case there are questions.

Where investigations are handled by an office external to the law enforcement agency, complaint files and related information would need to be transmitted to the department unit designated to secure and store files. Whether complaints are investigated internally or externally, copies of some case files may have to be provided to other governmental departments that require such information for related legal or disciplinary matters. For example, as discussed in Chapter 7.C.4., criminal prosecutors are required to disclose to a defendant materially exculpatory evidence, which could include sustained findings on particular types of misconduct allegations against an officer involved in the defendant's arrest. *Brady v. Maryland*, 373 U.S. 83 (1963). The investigative office should develop protocols to identify the circumstances and process by which it shares case files with other governmental entities.

COMPLAINT CLOSURE

- Review the case file for quality control.
- Update the electronic or other case tracking system.
- Notify the complainant and named officer of closure and findings.
- Transmit the investigative file to appropriate units within the law enforcement agency and other governmental offices, as required.
- Secure the file for later access, as needed.

I. Data Collection

Data collected from misconduct investigations provides valuable information about trends in police contacts that result in complaints. The investigative office should develop a systematized process that captures detailed information regarding pertinent aspects of the complaint, the underlying police incident, and the investigation and findings in such a way that the information can be tabulated, analyzed, and used to produce statistical reports and flag issues for further research and analysis. Data collection should start at the outset of the investigation and be updated through the closure process. Chapter 6.B. details some types of information that can be captured for study and reporting purposes.

Review Questions

1. What does "the standard of review" mean? Which standard is typically used in administrative investigations? Discuss reasons why this standard makes sense for misconduct cases.
2. In cases in which the only two witnesses disagree on the facts, how can the investigator resolve the conflicting evidence with a determinative finding; i.e., sustained, unfounded, or exonerated? What factors can be used to evaluate credibility?
3. What elements should be considered in recommending a particular level of discipline? Are there alternatives to unpaid time off as discipline? Why might these alternatives be good choices?
4. Why is it important to track a wide variety of complaint-related demographics, issues, and topics? How can this information be useful?

Notes

1 For an example of application of the IRAC approach, see Gareth Jones, *Conducting Administrative, Oversight & Ombudsman Investigations* (The Cartwright Group, 2009), beginning at p. 262.

2 For a sample template to use in organizing investigative evidence and findings, see Frank A. Colaprete, *Internal Investigations—A Practitioner's Approach* (Charles C. Thomas, 2007), Appendix A.

3 *Department of Justice Report Regarding the Criminal Investigation into the Shooting Death of Michael Brown by Ferguson, Missouri Police Officer Darren Wilson* (March 4, 2015), https://www.justice.gov/sites/default/files/opa/press-releases/attachments/2015/03/04/doj_report_on_shooting_of_michael_brown_1.pdf; and *Department of Justice Report on Investigation of the Ferguson Police Department* (March 4, 2015), https://www.justice.gov/sites/default/files/opa/press-releases/attachments/2015/03/04/ferguson_police_department_report.pdf

4 For information on use of Education Based Discipline in the Los Angeles County Sheriff's Department, see *Guidelines for Discipline Handbook* (Los Angeles County Sheriff's Department, Jim Mconnell, Sheriff, rev. January 1, 2017).

In Chapter 5

Special Issues in Investigating or Reviewing Police Misconduct Complaints

Chapter 5

Special Issues in Investigating or Reviewing Police Misconduct Complaints

While the majority of complaints will be processed in a standard manner, some cases will require special handling due to the size and breadth of the investigations, timeline issues, or complicated legal factors. Examples of matters that could possibly require special assignment or handling include: cases in which the investigative office has concurrent jurisdiction with another agency, complaints resulting from alleged civil rights or Equal Employment Opportunity (EEO) violations, complaints involving possible criminal misconduct allegations, allegations of biased policing, cases implicating officers' First Amendment rights, investigations resulting from large demonstrations or events with multiple related complaints, and misconduct allegations growing out of critical incidents. Also, as law enforcement rapidly changes in response to new technologies, complainants may raise concerns related to these developments, requiring that investigative office personnel stay informed about potential impacts of technological advances.

A. Concurrent Administrative Investigations

In jurisdictions in which an oversight agency has authority to conduct independent misconduct investigations concurrently with a law enforcement investigative office, it is necessary to develop protocols between the two offices to handle complaint processing. Policies should be developed that establish

OVERSIGHT INVOLVEMENT IN COMPLAINT ADJUDICATION

Oversight agencies fill a variety of roles in recommending or making findings and disciplinary decisions. Some examples of the types of authority include: (1) the oversight agency makes recommended findings (or recommended findings and discipline) and forwards the complaint to the law enforcement executive or city manager for a final decision; (2) the oversight agency makes determinative findings and the agency's attorney presents the case in a hearing before the law enforcement executive, city manager, or other authority who sets discipline; and (3) the findings of the oversight agency are presented to a civilian hearing examiner or commission for final decision. If a hearing is held, it may or may not be public, and the authority of a commission to adjudicate complaints may be dependent on the type of allegation or level of discipline involved.

If the law enforcement executive and the oversight agency disagree on findings in a particular case, some jurisdictions require that the disagreement be publicly reported and/or an appeal option be provided to resolve any dispute. No two oversight agency structures or processes are identical, and their authority and the steps involved in resolving misconduct complaints differ by jurisdiction.

timelines and procedures for communicating complaint receipt and the changing status of investigations, sharing of evidence, and deadlines for completing investigation reports and hearings (if applicable). Lines of authority should be explicitly delineated, and should include methods to resolve conflicting findings.

B. Complaints of Potential Civil Rights Violations or Other Claims

Some allegations of police misconduct may have related claims of civil rights violations, most commonly asserted under Section 1983 of the U.S. Code.[1] Section 1983 creates a federal cause of action for individuals who allege that they have been deprived of their rights, privileges, or immunities under the U.S. Constitution or federal statutes. For example, a complainant might assert a First Amendment violation under Section 1983, claiming they were illegally arrested while protesting at a political rally. While pursuing a civil claim seeking monetary damages for the alleged civil rights violation, they also could file an administrative misconduct complaint with the investigative office, alleging a violation of the police department's arrest policy, with the goal that the officer be disciplined or that demonstration policies be reformed.

Misconduct complaint investigations should move forward to a final disposition, even if a separate Section 1983 claim or other civil action has been filed. The complainant, subject officer, law enforcement agency, and community all have interests in seeing that misconduct is addressed or that the officer is exonerated, and that related departmental policies are reviewed and updated where appropriate—interests separate from compensation that may be sought by the complainant from a civil action.

While attorneys representing the complainant, officer, or other parties might seek detailed information during the investigation, protocols should be in place to provide only the most general status update until the investigation is completed and closed. Once the complaint is closed, however, parties to a civil action often seek a copy of the file through formal discovery, and could seek to depose the investigator or others from the investigative office or subpoena investigative personnel to testify at trial regarding the investigation and its outcome. It is important to consult with legal counsel for the investigative office before responding to any subpoena or discovery request.

C. Complaints Involving Potential Criminal Misconduct

Some complaints involve allegations that rise to the level of possible criminal misconduct. For example, an administrative allegation of excessive use of force also could be pursued criminally as aggravated assault or another criminal offense (and the complainant also may seek monetary damages via a civil lawsuit under Section 1983 or state law). When such a misconduct complaint is filed, an assessment must be made to determine whether the matter should be referred for criminal investigation and (potential) prosecution before the administrative investigation is conducted, whether the administrative investigation should proceed to determine if criminal misconduct appears to be at issue, or whether the administrative and criminal investigations should be handled concurrently. As noted in Chapter 3.C.4., and later discussed in Chapter 7.C.3., an officer's Fifth Amendment right against self-incrimination will become an issue if their *Garrity* compelled administrative statement is improperly used in subsequent criminal proceedings, in contravention of *Garrity* protections.

In some circumstances when an administrative complaint is filed there is no question that a criminal issue is involved, such as cases in which an officer has been arrested. Department policies may require that officers report if they are the subject of a criminal investigation, criminal traffic citation, arrest, or conviction. Officers also may have an affirmative duty to report other indications of possible criminal misconduct, such as being the respondent of a protection order, restraining order, or no contact order, having their driver license suspended or revoked, or if they are required to use an ignition interlock device. In such circumstances, the officer's supervisor or someone outside the department might initiate an administrative misconduct complaint related to the alleged criminal activity.

In other cases, it is not clear at the outset whether criminal misconduct is at issue. If the facts alleged would rise to a level of criminal misconduct if proven true, and the preliminary investigation supports the allegations, protocols should be in place to refer such cases to the appropriate authority for evaluation of any potential criminal matter involved. For example, an allegation that an officer took and discarded a bag of fast food the complainant purchased immediately before their arrest for possession with the intent to sell heroin, even if proven true, likely would not lead to criminal charges against the officer, though the administrative investigation could result in administrative discipline. However, an accusation that an officer pocketed a stack of bills, as witnessed and reported by another officer during an undercover drug raid where large quantities of heroin, cash, and guns were seized, if proven true, likely would result in criminal charges against the subject officer. In less clear cases, the investigative office may need to conduct further investigation to determine whether to refer the matter for review for criminal investigation.

PEER INTERVENTION CAN SAVE LIVES AND CAREERS

Police peer intervention training teaches officers, in a practical and positive way, the powerful influence that they can have on the conduct of their fellow officers. The training equips and supports officers to perform interventions to prevent their colleagues from committing acts of serious or potentially criminal misconduct. By learning "critical loyalty," how to recognize situations that require ethical decision making, and how to successfully intervene, officers are taught to be prepared psychologically and tactically, and to understand that peer intervention is a vital part of their professional duty and essential for their own survival. The New Orleans Police Department (NOPD) adopted a peer intervention program called Ethical Policing is Courageous (EPIC) that has been viewed as an important part of positive change in NOPD. The program is being adopted by other law enforcement agencies.[2]

Given that criminal misconduct issues might arise, investigative offices should develop policies and procedures for determining whether an administrative investigation will be conducted concurrently, sequentially (with the administrative matter stayed until the criminal process is completed), or handled on a case-by-case basis. The goals and purposes behind the criminal and administrative processes are different, as are the standards of proof, as discussed in Chapter 2.A. Consequently, the issue of whether to conduct concurrent investigations requires critical thinking about the pros and cons involved. Ideally, the investigative office will have flexibility to determine when to move forward concurrently and when to wait for the outcome of the criminal process.

Some issues to consider in developing guidelines for whether or not to conduct an administrative investigation concurrent with the criminal process include:

- Waiting until the criminal process is completed can mean significant delays for the administrative investigation. Culpable officers are not disciplined expeditiously and those who should be exonerated do not have their names cleared in a timely manner.
- Delayed investigations can reflect negatively on the investigative office and law enforcement agency. The general public may not understand the complexity of issues involved and experience

frustration with the time-consuming nature of the process, particularly if an officer receives pay while on an extended administrative leave.

- If the administrative investigation is postponed, witnesses may become unavailable, memories may fade, and statements may change over time, resulting in reliability or credibility issues. However, an investigative office should be able to rely on evidence gathered in the criminal investigation, mitigating the impact of these issues.
- If discipline is imposed based on an administrative investigation prior to the conclusion of the criminal process, plea bargaining or a criminal trial outcome ultimately could impact the officer's ability to work. The law enforcement agency could then be prevented from taking further administrative action by law or a collective bargaining contract.
- If a compelled administrative statement is taken prior to the completion of the criminal process, the officer might argue that other evidence from the investigation should be suppressed during criminal proceedings, as having been discovered or developed as a result of the officer's statement, even if the statement is withheld.

TIMING DISCIPLINE WITH THE CRIMINAL INVESTIGATION

When an officer is under criminal investigation, procedural issues can arise with any related administrative discipline. For example, if an officer is arrested for Driving Under the Influence and disciplined with a suspension for a set number of days, the criminal process might later result in a requirement that the officer drive with an interlock device. Assuming the department would refuse to install such a device on a patrol car or allow the officer to drive with a restricted license, it could determine they cannot perform the duties required of patrol officers. In light of the earlier suspension, the question is whether the officer later can be terminated for work limitations growing out of the same incident for which discipline had already been imposed.

In proceeding with a parallel administrative investigation, the investigative office must ensure that its investigation does not impede the criminal case. If a *Garrity* protected administrative interview of the subject officer is conducted before the criminal proceedings are concluded, the investigative office must guard against releasing the statement for use in a criminal prosecution. One safeguard would be to place the officer's statement in a sealed envelope, with the case number and contents identified on the outside, along with a notation that the statement is *Garrity* protected. While a criminal prosecutor likely could access the administrative investigation, the *Garrity* protected statement should be withheld, though its existence would be noted in the transmission memorandum. Administrative investigative office personnel must be properly trained regarding the legal issues involved and consultation with legal counsel might be necessary in a specific case, to ensure compliance with *Garrity* procedures for protection of self-incriminating testimony. See the discussions in Chapter 3.C.4. and Chapter 7.C.3.

Agencies must weigh many factors when criminal charges against an officer are at issue. If there are no set protocols, the decision as to whether to conduct concurrent or sequential investigations when criminal misconduct is alleged should be made on a case-by-case basis. If the decision is made to stay the administrative investigation, there should be tracking mechanisms in place to ensure that the investigation is conducted in a timely manner and discipline is imposed, as appropriate, once the criminal case is completed.

D. Complaints Involving Equal Employment Opportunity Matters

Under federal law, employment discrimination based on race, color, religion, sex (including pregnancy), national origin, age (40+), disability or genetic information, or retaliation for filing a complaint of discrimination, is illegal. A discrimination claim based on any of these protected classes often is referred to as an Equal Employment Opportunity (EEO) complaint.[3] State and local laws also may provide protections against discrimination based on these and other categories, such as marital or parental status. Further, federal, state, and local laws, and many law enforcement agencies also prohibit workplace harassment tied to membership in a protected class, including sexual harassment.

Some investigative offices handling police misconduct complaints do not investigate EEO claims by an employee against the law enforcement agency where they work, as there are unique procedural and proof issues involved. Protocols should be established to refer these complaints to the proper agency or departmental unit responsible for EEO cases within the jurisdiction. Investigative offices that do handle EEO allegations should ensure investigators assigned to these cases have specialized training in the issues involved. Investigative offices should develop tracking mechanisms for EEO complaints that are referred elsewhere to monitor whether misconduct issues emerge as EEO issues are investigated or if there is a pattern of EEO complaints that could require a separate misconduct investigation.

E. Complaints Alleging Biased Policing

Biased policing complaints concern enforcement action, inaction, or the use of offensive language or slurs by a law enforcement employee based on race, ethnicity, national origin, gender, sexual preference, or other protected classification. The terms "biased policing" and "racial profiling" often are used interchangeably. Biased policing, real or perceived, can undermine public trust in law enforcement and complaints must be thoroughly investigated and tracked to determine if there is individual misconduct or if there are patterns in allegations of bias.

Biased policing complaints can involve difficult proof issues, complicated by the fact that police can legally act on suspect profile descriptions that include race, gender, age, and other descriptors. Often there are no witnesses in biased policing cases other than the named officer and the person alleging misconduct. In such cases, it is particularly important that the investigator strive to determine if either the officer or the complainant is more credible, using the credibility assessment approaches discussed in Chapter 4.B.

Biased policing allegations may be particularly appropriate for mediation or another alternative dispute resolution (ADR) program, as a facilitated discussion between the complainant and the named officer can help each understand the other's perspective about the incident. The investigative office should develop explicit criteria for determining which bias complaints could benefit from referral to such programs. For more discussion on mediation and ADR see Chapter 2.E.

Some investigative offices are involved in investigations of bias in a particular operational unit or throughout the law enforcement organization. For example, along with investigating specific incidents of alleged bias in traffic stops or arrests, data may be collected and analyzed to determine if there is quantitative evidence that community members of a particular racial or ethnic group are stopped or arrested at significantly higher rates than others. This process is complicated by issues of statistical reliability and factors such as the populations used in making comparisons. It is essential that personnel have expertise in conducting audits or systemic investigations, or that the investigative office involve experts to analyze the issues and data.

POLICE INTERACTIONS WITH TRANSGENDER, NON-BINARY, AND GENDER NON-CONFORMING PEOPLE

There have been efforts in law enforcement organizations across the U.S. to enact policies and procedures to protect the dignity and safety of LGBTQ+ individuals, as victims of crime, suspects, or otherwise. For example, New Jersey issued a directive in November 2019 that requires all state, county, and local law enforcement officers to treat a person based on their gender identity, regardless of gender assigned at birth. Among other requirements, the directive mandates that officers should not subject persons to invasive searches because of their identity or sexual orientation and should not inquire about anatomy or sexual practices, unless necessary for a criminal investigation.[4]

F. Complaints Involving Social Media Postings by Officers

Law enforcement regularly uses social media to communicate with the public, provide emergency alerts, or to investigate crimes. However, an officer's use of social media has the potential to reflect negatively on their department and the law enforcement profession in general, undercutting public trust and confidence. Posts and comments that are critical of the law enforcement agency, or racist, sexist, or otherwise patently offensive, have resulted in discipline, including termination, for some officers. Many departments have developed policies and training on internet usage, clarifying conduct expectations when using both departmental social media and personal accounts. A social media policy should recognize that officers' right of freedom of expression under the First Amendment must be balanced against the law enforcement department's interest in its public safety mission. This is a developing area of the law and consultation with legal counsel is advised when investigating complaints alleging that an officer violated a social media policy.

G. Video/Audio Complaint Evidence from In-Car and Body Cameras

Many law enforcement departments are using cameras to enhance accountability of officers' interactions with members of the public. While in-car camera systems have been used by law enforcement since the 1980s, body cameras have been adopted more recently by numerous agencies. Body cameras, generally worn on the officer's chest or hat, and in-car camera systems increase transparency and accountability by capturing video and audio during enforcement interactions. There are significant costs associated with storing and publicly disclosing recordings, as well as potential privacy concerns that must be considered as well. While research results are mixed as to whether police cameras reduce use of force or misconduct complaints, video/audio recordings can provide evidence allowing the investigative office to more quickly determine whether or not a complaint has merit.[5] A department's adoption of an in-car or body camera system likely will result in new conduct expectations related to camera usage and potential complaint processing issues, such as:

- The types of incidents that require mandatory recording and when officers have discretion to turn cameras (or the audio function) on or off.
- Whether officers are allowed to review recordings before completing incident reports.
- Whether officers are allowed to review recordings of an incident before being interviewed for a related misconduct investigation.

THE ROLE OF VIDEO AND AUDIO RECORDINGS IN THE LAQUAN McDONALD CASE

In 2014, Chicago Police Officer Jason Van Dyke shot and killed Laquan McDonald, a 17-year-old African American youth. Officers were responding to reports of vehicle break-ins when Van Dyke repeatedly shot McDonald shortly after arriving on-scene. Investigative reports by the Chicago Office of Inspector General, the United States Department of Justice, and others illustrate how use of video/audio recordings by law enforcement played an important role in determining findings. First, though Van Dyke initially stated that McDonald lunged at him with a knife and that he moved to increase the distance between himself and McDonald before shooting him, in-car camera (and a security camera) video contradicted that account. Second, video footage helped to determine other officers' placement at the scene, providing proof that they lied when claiming they heard Van Dyke tell McDonald to drop his weapon. Third, Van Dyke and other officers failed to ensure their in-car cameras were working properly to record both video and audio, as policy required. Finally, the Chicago Police Department failed to release camera footage until it was court-ordered, a year after McDonald's shooting. The delay and lack of transparency were viewed by many as increasing the community's perception of a cover-up and fuelling the widespread protests that followed.[6]

Law enforcement organizations using body or in-car cameras should develop policies that address these and other procedural issues before camera usage is made mandatory, providing officers and investigative offices with clear guidelines on camera usage expectations. There also should be explicit timelines for retention of video/audio recordings and protocols for public release of recordings.

H. Complaints Related to Demonstrations and Other Large Events

Demonstrations and other large public events can present a challenge to law enforcement. These incidents can put agencies in the media limelight and bring scrutiny to police tactics used to manage crowds. In some instances, multiple agencies are called in to provide mutual assistance for policing large events. Law enforcement agencies should train officers in constitutional policing of demonstrations, conduct pre-event planning to anticipate issues where possible, and have clear protocols regarding chain of command in mutual aid situations.

Investigations of complaints resulting from large events can present unique issues. Multiple complaints may be filed about the same or different incidents related to the event, officers from different agencies can be involved, and officer and witness identification can be challenging. These cases can be complex and may require assignment of more than one investigator to ensure that the

OFFICER IDENTIFICATION

All law enforcement agencies should require officers to wear visible name tags and badge numbers on all outward facing garments. Some departments, such as the San Francisco Police Department, also require officers to prominently display badge numbers on helmets during demonstrations to assist in officer identification.

investigation is completed in a timely manner, or may call for coordination between investigators or different investigative offices to share multiple perspectives in evaluating the evidence.

I. Critical Incident Roll Out

Investigative offices may be authorized to roll out to the scene of critical incidents, such as officer-involved shootings or problematic high speed pursuits. Protocols should be developed detailing how the police department will notify the investigative office when such incidents occur, and who is responsible for doing so. Having the ability to immediately assess the layout of the incident site, identify possible witnesses, and observe the criminal or other administrative investigation as it occurs will help facilitate the investigation of any misconduct complaint subsequently filed.

J. Regular Review of Claims and Litigation for Misconduct Issues

Investigative offices should have protocols in place to consider claims and litigation regarding law enforcement incidents in case a matter involves potential misconduct, but has not been filed as an administrative complaint. Setting up a system to regularly review these actions ensures that misconduct does not go unaddressed and provides an opportunity to flag potential policy or training issues, as well. It is helpful for the investigative office to establish good communications with local, state, and federal attorneys who may discover potential misconduct as they investigate, prosecute, or defend actions and can refer such matters for administrative review. As discussed in Section B. of this chapter, investigative offices should proceed with investigating a complaint even though there is a related civil action moving forward, as there are different, though sometimes overlapping, interests involved, and different timelines for completion.

K. Technological Advances

Technological advances provide opportunities for law enforcement to increase its effectiveness and improve public safety. However, these advances can result in new types of misconduct allegations (e.g., that the technology is unreliable or infringes on civil rights) or create procedural issues when insufficient attention is paid to creating policies and procedures for use of new technology.

New technologies available to law enforcement for surveillance, searches, and criminal investigations raise a variety of concerns regarding the potential for civil rights and privacy violations in the digital age. Through rapidly developing digital technologies, law enforcement agencies have access to programs and equipment that can collect and analyze information on people without their knowledge. Some examples of these technologies include: (1) cell phone tracking and listening devices; (2) drones and other remotely or autonomously powered systems used for surveillance, search and rescue, and additional law enforcement purposes; (3) automatic license plate readers/recognition devices that capture and store license plate data on vehicles passing within a range, recording the time, date, and location; and (4) biometric systems used to capture, analyze, and match a person's physical or biological features, such as facial recognition technology.

The investigative office should be planning for and responding to the unique issues that may develop relating to methods of collection, retention, and use of data associated with technological changes made in their jurisdiction. Furthermore, misconduct investigators themselves increasingly may turn to using data mining techniques, such as using facial recognition from video footage to assist in identifying a witness, or sifting through digital evidence on a named officer's cell phone or computer to locate evidence relevant to a misconduct complaint. The investigative office should be cognizant of limitations in using a particular technology and consider whether the possibility of bias or privacy infringement outweighs any potential benefit for the investigation process.

Review Questions

1. What kinds of protocols should be developed when there is more than one office with jurisdiction to investigate misconduct complaints involving the same law enforcement organization?
2. When misconduct involves both criminal and administrative issues, what issues should be considered in deciding whether to conduct a concurrent administrative investigation or to postpone the administrative review until after the criminal process is completed?
3. What advantages are there to having investigative office personnel roll out to critical incident investigations?
4. Discuss ways that advances in policing technology can result in new types of misconduct complaints.

Notes

1 42 U.S.C. Section 1983: Civil Action for Deprivation of Rights.
2 Jonathan Aronie and Christy E. Lopez, "Keeping Each Other Safe: An Assessment of the Use of Peer Intervention Programs to Prevent Police Officer Mistakes and Misconduct, Using New Orleans' EPIC Program as a Potential National Model," *Police Quarterly* 20(3) (September 2017): 295–321.
3 42 U.S.C. Section 2000e-2: Unlawful Employment Practices.
4 Attorney General Law Enforcement Directive No 2019-3: Law Enforcement Interactions with Transgender Individuals (November 20, 2019), https://www.nj.gov/oag/dcj/directiv.htm
5 Cynthia Lum, Megan Stoltz, Christopher S. Koper, and J. Amber Scherer, "Research on Body-Worn Cameras: What We Know, What We Need to Know," *Criminology & Public Policy* 18 (2019): 93–118, https://doi.org/10.1111/1745-9133.12412
6 *Summary Report of Investigation, Office of Inspector General, Case #15-0564 (Officer Jason Van Dyke)* (June 30, 2016).

In Chapter 6

Reporting Out

Statistics, Recommendations, and More

A. Statistical Reports
B. Examples of Data and Issues to Track
   1. Complaint Demographics and Investigation Issues
   2. Use of Force-Related Tracking Issues
   3. Search-Related Tracking Issues
   4. Additional Topics for Tracking
C. Reporting on Policy and Training Recommendations
D. Use of Reports to Illustrate the Investigation Process

Chapter 6

Reporting Out

Statistics, Recommendations, and More

Writing and disseminating periodic reports about the work of the investigative office informs stakeholders about trends in complaint issues, policy and training changes, and outreach efforts. Such reports should convey to the public, government officials, and the law enforcement department any important conclusions to be drawn from the data. In addition to annual reporting, some investigative offices issue more frequent reports, allowing for timely discussion of specific topics of interest to stakeholders and intermittent information on case processing. Ideally, reports should be available in hard copy and posted on the investigative office and department websites, with copies or an electronic link distributed to primary stakeholders in the area.

A. Statistical Reports

Statistical or analytic reports provide a means for public disclosure of issues related to the complaint investigation process. Complaint tracking databases or spreadsheets should be used to record and compile all data needed for analysis and reports to be published by the investigative office. Information reported should be summarized and explained, with charts, graphs, and other tools used to make it easy to understand and accessible to the larger community. Presenting multi-year data comparisons is necessary to observe and track trends in complaints and other issues. While most departments may have too small a data set to draw statistically significant conclusions, efforts can still be made to identify relevant trends.

Research analyzing police misconduct complaints is limited. One study of misuse of force complaints concluded that it is difficult to conduct research of complaint handling across departments for a variety of reasons, including agency specific complaint processes, codes of conduct, policies and procedures, and degrees of internal/external review.[1] Nonetheless, investigative offices should develop tracking systems to observe changes over time within their jurisdiction, bearing in mind that the size of the department and number of misconduct complaints handled may limit the ability to make statistically reliable observations.

Based on state statutes and negotiated contracts, many jurisdictions are required to maintain confidentiality of complaint information, such as the identity of named officers and their disciplinary records. Agencies bound by confidentiality requirements should issue statistical reports that provide detailed aggregate complaint information. Illustrative narratives about complaints can be developed to provide more insight on concerns raised, without sacrificing confidentiality.

MAKE STATISTICS RELEVANT

Issuing periodic reports analyzing complaint data and outcomes is an opportunity for the investigative office to provide transparency and garner feedback and stakeholder support. Press releases may encourage coverage of the report in the local media.

Information about complaint trends and policy changes should be written to explain the impact of the issues, if possible. For example: have complaints increased in a particular district? If so, that could point to a need for outreach, retraining, or community mediation. If complaints of officer rudeness have declined, was this the result of a change in policy or targeted training?

Investigative offices can report on all stakeholder outreach conducted during the reporting period. It also is useful to report on information and insights gained from training and networking with investigative staff from other jurisdictions.

Statistical reports can include a wide variety of information regarding complaints and investigations. Some examples of complaint data and information typically reported include:

- Number of complaints filed
- Number and types of allegations received
- Case classification distribution
- Number of investigations closed
- Types of allegations and findings in closed cases
- Complaint trends in comparison to the same period in previous years
- Number of cases resulting in each of the possible findings
- Nature of disciplinary action taken in sustained cases
- Geographic, racial, ethnic, age, and gender distribution of complainants and officers
- Number of officers who have received multiple and sustained complaints within the reporting period
- Years of employment of subject officers and officers with sustained complaints
- Timeliness of complaint handling
- Information about cases referred for mediation or alternative dispute resolution
- Summaries of cases in which there was agreement/disagreement as they are reviewed by the chain of command, or where appealed

Collecting and regularly updating data from the outset of an investigation through closure facilitates access to the information necessary for thorough and timely reports. Complaints are important quality control indicators, and the wealth of data they contain, if properly gathered and analyzed, provides invaluable information for police commanders and government officials to identify potential areas for remediation.

This data can identify specific practices, such as discretionary arrests or search-related tactics, which could give rise to complaints, along with specific units or commands where patterns of police–civilian interactions merit closer examination. Complaint history should be seen as one of many factors in the assessment of an officer, unit, or specialty team—an indicator as to how officers are handling interactions with members of the public.

B. Examples of Data and Issues to Track

Developing a database of a wide range of incident-related details is key to the investigative office having the ability to research issues quickly and accurately if there are questions about a complaint or similar incidents at a later time. A comprehensive database also allows for trend analysis and statistical reporting. The data tracking system should be updated upon complaint receipt, during the investigation, and at closure. Issues and topics to consider tracking include:

1. Complaint Demographics and Investigation Issues

- Investigator name
- Supervisor name
- Complainant name and contact information (and back-up contact information, if possible)
- Complainant race, ethnicity, and gender
- Officer name, badge number, unit, and work shift
- Officer race, ethnicity, and gender
- Day and time of incident underlying complaint
- Location of incident by address and agency precinct/district
- Nature of police contact: call for service, on-view, traffic related, other
- Allegations and findings
- Identity and contact information for all witnesses interviewed
- Charges filed in underlying incident
    - Discretionary charges filed: resisting arrest, obstruction, public intoxication, other
    - Most serious charge filed
- Issues not investigated or dropped without finding
- Investigation timeline compliance
- Interview/document access delays
- Mediation or other dispute resolution

2. Use of Force-Related Tracking Issues

- Complainant armed: firearm, knife, other
- Complainant mental health concerns, under the influence, other
- Crisis intervention or mental health practitioners called or on-scene
- Death: complainant, officer, both, other
- De-escalation techniques used
- High speed pursuit
- Force alleged consistent with force reported, any differences noted
- Force documentation: completed, reviewed, approved
- Force used
    - Canine bite
    - Chemical weapon: pepper spray, tear gas, mace, or other
    - Electronic Control Weapon (ECW): probe, drive-stun; number and length of activations
    - Firearm: drawn and pointed, discharged, number of discharges
    - Force after handcuffing

- Handcuffing issue/injury
  - Impact force: baton or other
  - Location of force: face, head, neck, torso, genitals, limbs
  - Physical/bodily force: elbow, feet, hands, head, knees, control hold
  - Takedown: against car, wall, ground, or other
- Injuries
  - Complainant injuries: visible, photographed, medical attention
  - Officer injuries: visible, photographed, medical attention
- Medical attention: emergency medical technician (EMT), hospital transport, follow-up medical care
- Medical records: consent to release, records collected, significant delays
- Vehicle impact
- Verbal orders given

3. *Search-Related Tracking Issues*

- Place/person/object searched
  - Documents
  - Electronic device: cellphone, computer, other
  - Person: pat-down/frisk, body cavity search
  - Personal effects: purse, backpack, briefcase, suitcase, other
  - Recordings
  - Residence, business, other
  - Vehicle
- Record of evidence seized, if any
- Search pursuant to warrant
- Search pursuant to warrant exceptions
  - Consent search - evidence of consent: e.g., signed consent form, video/audio recording of consent
  - Emergency doctrine and community care exception
  - Hot pursuit
  - Inventory search
  - Open view search
  - Plain view search
  - Probation/parole search
  - Search incident to arrest

4. *Additional Topics for Tracking*

- Americans with Disabilities (ADA) access violation
- Alcohol/public intoxication/driving under the influence
- Biased policing
- Bicycle: stop, citation, or accident
- Car accident
- Car tow

JURISDICTION SPECIFIC TRACKING

Unique issues within a jurisdiction may result in prioritizing particular types of data to track. For example, new case law may lead investigative offices in Oregon to more closely track complaints related to vehicle searches during traffic stops. In a decision out of the Oregon Supreme Court, a driver was pulled over for failing to signal a turn. As testified was routine practice, the officer asked the driver whether there was anything illegal in the vehicle and whether a search could be made for "guns, drugs, knives, bombs, illegal documents, or anything else you're not allowed to possess." The driver consented to a search and the officer discovered methamphetamine on the floor of the car. The Court determined that the questions asked of the driver and search were impermissible under the Oregon Constitution, since a motorist stopped for a traffic infraction is not free to leave, in contrast to officer/pedestrian investigatory stops. Officers must keep their activities and questions "reasonably related" to the purpose of making the traffic stop, unless a separate basis for reasonable suspicion becomes evident during the stop. *Oregon v. Arreola-Botello*, Docket Number: S066119 (Nov. 15, 2019).

- Civil standby
- Curb sitting or kneeling
- Curfew
- Derogatory words
- Discretionary arrest
- Display of force
- Domestic violence
- Drug/substance impairment or use
- Excessive deployment
- Failure to process rape kit
- Field Training Officer (FTO)
- First Amendment violation
- Fleeing suspect
- Gang issues
- High risk stop
- Homeless
- Informant
- Jaywalking or crosswalk violation
- Lesbian/gay/bisexual/transgender/queer/questioning (LGBTQ+)
- Loitering
- Missing/damaged property
- Nightclub
- Non-English speaking
- Officer arrest
- Officer identification issue
- Officer off-duty

- Officer retirement or resignation following complaint
- Onlooker or bystander arrest
- Pretext stop
- Probationary officer/recruit
- Profanity or rudeness
- Prone handcuffing
- Protestors or demonstration
- Racial slur
- Resisting arrest
- Restraining order
- Retaliation
- School campus
- Secondary employment
- Sexual misconduct
- Sports event
- Surveillance issue
- Tight handcuffs
- Traffic stop
- Trespassing
- Vehicle citation
- Welfare check

The suggestions presented here may or may not be relevant in a particular jurisdiction and other issues may come to the forefront over time. Identifying pertinent issues at the outset helps ensure that the investigative office collects the appropriate data for analysis.

C. Reporting on Policy and Training Recommendations

Regardless of findings made on complaint allegations, an investigation could point to broader policy or training issues, or the need for attention to staffing, equipment, or tactical matters. Policy and other recommended changes in policing procedures can result in some of the most lasting, influential work of an investigative office. Recommendations can be relevant to a particular officer, unit, precinct, or the entire law enforcement agency.

It may be beneficial for the department to collaborate on some policy development or training revisions stemming from investigative office recommendations by establishing a working group including community members and outside subject matter experts. For example, the collaborative model has been used in a number of jurisdictions as they adopt body cameras. Public confidence in policing can be enhanced through such inclusive projects.[2]

Protocols should be in place to track recommendations and ensure proper follow-up. It is important to track all recommendations with notes indicating when each was made, whether there are relationships among recommendations, and listing relevant details about specific cases involved, and chronicling the review process.

Policy and training recommendations can bring about important improvements to the law enforcement agency and should be a focal point in the investigative office's reporting to stakeholders. Information reported by the investigative office can highlight each recommendation, the rationale behind the recommendation, and the law enforcement agency's response, including implementation or other results.

MONITORING POLICY AND TRAINING CHANGES—LESSONS FROM ERIC GARNER'S DEATH

In 2014, Eric Garner, a 43-year-old African American father of six, was apprehended by New York Police Department (NYPD) officers, accused of selling loose cigarettes. As seen in the recorded incident, which received widespread media attention, Officer Daniel Panatelo held Garner in a chokehold as Garner was heard crying out, "I can't breathe." Garner died later at an area hospital.

Eric Garner's death prompted a review of chokehold cases by the NYPD Inspector General (OIG-NYPD). The NYPD use of force policy had banned chokeholds over 20 years previously. However, the OIG-NYPD noted that the Civilian Complaint Review Board had recorded rising numbers of complaints of chokeholds being used as of 2013. Although OIG-NYPD's review was limited in scope and need for further study was indicated, the report concluded that NYPD discipline for the use of chokeholds was very low or non-existent. Also, OIG-NYPD found that officers used chokeholds before first using lower level force, raising concerns about training on acceptable use of force and de-escalation techniques.[3]

D. Use of Reports to Illustrate the Investigation Process

The investigation process can be confusing to many, and investigative office reports can be an opportunity to describe how misconduct complaints are handled. For example, the report could provide scenarios to illustrate the complaint classification system; e.g., the types of cases most likely referred to a supervisor, verses those that will be handled by the investigative office, or those that are appropriate for mediation. Similarly, a discussion about the range of investigation outcomes could define each possible finding and include sample case facts illustrating each determination. The scenarios used could be fictional or drawn from actual complaints that were investigated, to the extent that confidentiality can be preserved.

Review Questions

1. What are the benefits of issuing periodic complaint reports to the community?
2. Name some ways that tracking detailed information mined from complaint investigations can provide a department with information to identify possible issues with training or personnel.
3. Discuss how policy development can benefit from collaboration with stakeholders. Which stakeholders could be included in such working groups?

Notes

1 Mathew Hickman and Jane Poore, "National Data on Citizen Complaints About Police Use of Force: Data Quality Concerns and the Potential (Mis)use of Statistical Evidence to Address Police Agency Conduct," *Criminal Justice Policy Review* 27 (2016): 455–79.

2 Maria Ponomarenko and Barry Friedman, "Democratic Accountability and Policing," *Reforming Criminal Justice* 2 (2017).

3 New York City Department of Investigation, Office of the Inspector General for the NYPD. *Observations on Accountability and Transparency in Ten NYPD Chokehold Cases* (January 2015).

In Chapter 7

Personnel and Training Considerations

A. Investigation Skills Training
   1. Misconduct Investigation Basics
   2. Law Enforcement Department Standards and Procedures
   3. Transparency and Accountability for the Investigative Office
B. Training Resources
C. Examples of Legal Issues Relevant to Police Misconduct Investigations
   1. Use of Force
   2. Stops, Searches, and In-Custody Questioning
   3. Misconduct Complaint Investigation Procedures
   4. Disclosure of Investigation Materials for Criminal Proceedings

Chapter 7

Personnel and Training Considerations

Individuals handling police misconduct complaints, including investigators, supervisors, and executive personnel, require developed knowledge and skills to produce timely, thorough investigations and effective office management to ensure the highest performance and integrity standards. A well-functioning investigative office also works to enhance its relationship with all stakeholders, including complainants, law enforcement department commanders and officers, the community, and government officials.

A. Investigation Skills Training

Training should be developed for personnel with different roles and skill levels; e.g., orientation for new investigators and other staff, regular in-service training for all staff, and individualized training plans to address employee-specific development. General and specialized training opportunities can be found locally and on state and national levels, and offer the chance to network with others working with police misconduct issues. A list of sample organizations offering information and training relevant to misconduct complaint investigations is provided in Section B., following the lists immediately below of suggested training topics.

1. Misconduct Investigation Basics

- Administrative investigations of officer-involved shootings and other critical incidents
- *Brady* requirements for coordinating with prosecutors regarding misconduct investigation materials
- Communication with subject officers, complainants, and witnesses
- Credibility evaluations
- Data tracking
- *Garrity* advisements
- Implicit bias
- Intake, complaint classification, findings, and discipline procedures
- Interview skills
- Investigation and discipline timelines
- Investigation plans and use of witness/evidence matrixes
- Investigative office policies and standard operating procedures
- Mediation and other alternative dispute resolution options
- Medical records: consent for release, retrieval, and analysis
- Preservation of evidence

- Retrieval and analysis of law enforcement agency documents and communications records
- Retrieval and analysis of video/audio recordings: in-car, body, cell phone, holding cell, and private or law enforcement surveillance systems
- Summary and analysis of evidence, findings, policy/training recommendations, and report writing

2. *Law Enforcement Department Standards and Procedures*

- Biased policing policy
- Collective bargaining agreement provisions that apply to complaint investigations, discipline, and appeal processes
- Criminal investigation processes including for instance, domestic violence, sexual assault, homicide, and other critical incidents
- Crisis intervention protocols and resources
- Early intervention program
- Law enforcement agency tactics and training concerning patrol; stops; search and seizure; arrests; prisoner transport; property and evidence processing; and policing demonstrations
- Law enforcement agency policy manual and other orders or directives regarding conduct expectations
- Mutual aid protocols between the law enforcement agency and other local agencies
- Officer involved shooting investigations and review
- Relevant federal, state, and local laws
- Use of force policy, training, reporting, and review (including de-escalation expectations)

In addition to training on the specific topics noted here, if the investigative office is outside the police department, personnel will need an orientation to the department's organizational structure and the work of all departmental units.

3. *Transparency and Accountability for the Investigative Office*

- Reporting on the work of the investigative office
- Strategies to engage and educate the public and law enforcement personnel about investigations, complaint processing, and policy development

B. Training Resources

Though there are many avenues for investigation training, the following list provides some examples of resources particularly relevant to the work of police misconduct investigations. Some of the resources listed are intended primarily for law enforcement personnel, while others focus more on civilians; however there is benefit to attending training offered through both channels to gain a wide perspective of the issues involved. A number of the organizations listed offer free and e-learning options and regular electronic informational updates. Details can be found by visiting the organization's website:

- American Civil Liberties Union (ACLU)
  www.aclu.org
- Americans for Effective Law Enforcement Legal Center (AELE)
  www.aele.org
- Association of Inspectors General (AIG)
  www.inspectorsgeneral.org

- Attorney associations at the federal, state, and local levels
- California Defense Investigators Association (CDIA)
  www.cdia.org
- Canadian Association for Civilian Oversight of Law Enforcement (CACOLE)
  www.cacole.ca/home-accueil-eng.shtml
- Community Oriented Policing Services (COPS), U.S. Department of Justice
  www.cops.usdoj.gov
- Daigle Law Group, LLC (a private law firm that issues legal updates and offers training)
  www.daiglelawgroup.com
- Fair and Impartial Policing
  www.fairimpartialpolicing.com
- Force Science Institute
  www.forcescience.org
- Immigrant rights groups, such as:
  - American Immigration Council (AIC)
    www.americanimmigrationcouncil.org
  - Northwest Immigrant Rights Project (NIRP)
    www.nwirp.org
- International Association of Chiefs of Police (IACP)
  www.theiacp.org
- International Law Enforcement Auditors Association (ILEAA)
  www.ileaa.org
- Museum of Tolerance: Tools for Tolerance for Law Enforcement and Criminal Justice
  www.museumoftolerance.com
- National Alliance on Mental Illness (NAMI)
  www.nami.org
- National Association for the Advancement of Colored People (NAACP)
  www.naacp.org
- National Association for Civilian Oversight of Law Enforcement (NACOLE)
  www.nacole.org
- National Defender Investigator Association (NDIA)
  www.ndia.net
- National Institute of Justice (NIJ)
  www.nij.gov/Pages/welcome.aspx
- National Organization of Black Law Enforcement Executives (NOBLE)
  www.noblenational.org
- National Police Accountability Project (NPAP)
  www.nlg-npap.org
- Police Executive Research Forum (PERF)
  www.policeforum.org
- Police Foundation
  www.policefoundation.org
- Public defender office(s) in the jurisdiction
- Southern Poverty Law Center (SPLC)
  www.splcenter.org

- State law enforcement training academies, such as:
  - California Commission on Peace Officers Standards and Training (POST) www.post.ca.gov
  - Washington State Criminal Justice Training Commission (WSCJTC) www.cjtc.state.wa.us

C. Examples of Legal Issues Relevant to Police Misconduct Investigations

Everyone involved with conducting or reviewing police misconduct complaints should be familiar with seminal legal decisions relevant to common allegations and investigation procedures. The law is constantly changing and it is imperative that investigative offices develop a process to keep updated on new legislation and changing case law, as well as related police agency policy revisions.

THE CHANGING LEGAL LANDSCAPE

Misconduct complaint investigators must be well informed about legal standards that impact how police enforce the law within the bounds of the U.S. Constitution, state and local mandates, and police agency policies. Legal cases and statutory authority discussed in the *Manual* provide only a starting point in analyzing a complaint in the context of legal and policy requirements in a particular jurisdiction, which may be more restrictive. Investigative offices should have access to counsel to ensure accurate analysis of legal issues involved in conducting misconduct investigations.

The following sections provide a few examples of the many legal issues relevant to handling misconduct investigations. The overview is neither intended to be legal advice regarding any particular issue, nor a full analysis of the cases listed. Each investigative office should have a legal advisor to keep abreast of the rapidly changing law in their jurisdiction.

1. Use of Force

Graham v. Connor, 490 U.S. 386 (1989): Under the Fourth Amendment, the "reasonableness" of a use of force by a police officer is judged from the perspective of a "reasonable officer on the scene," rather than the "20/20 vision of hindsight." The test of reasonableness is "not capable of precise definition or mechanical application." Consider the "totality of the circumstances" to evaluate each use of force applied to determine if it was reasonable and necessary by reviewing the following four factors: (1) What was the severity of the crime the officer believed the suspect had committed or was committing? (2) Did the suspect pose an immediate threat to the safety of the officer or others? (3) Was the suspect actively resisting arrest? (4) Was the suspect attempting to evade arrest by flight?

Courts have refined the *Graham* test in the 30 years since the decision, considering a range of factors such as the degree of threat posed by the suspect in light of the number of officers present, the role of immediately available less-lethal tools, and the impact of the suspect's level of impairment. In investigating the specific facts involved in an allegation of misuse of force, the *Graham* factors should be considered in light of federal court decisions subsequent to *Graham*, requirements under state law, and the law enforcement department's policies, which could set a more restrictive standard for

THE DEVELOPMENT OF HIGHER USE OF FORCE STANDARDS

Changes in use of force standards are developing at the state and local levels. For example, in 2019, Washington State and California both modified state laws regarding use of force. Washington redefined the standard for assessing use of deadly force and enacted other new requirements, including independent investigations of deadly force use. California's legislative changes include the requirement that lethal force be used only when necessary, and use of force review will consider the conduct of both the involved officer and subject leading up to the use of deadly force. The new statutes undoubtedly will undergo refinement as they are applied and challenged in court.

In another example of changing standards, in 2016, the Police Executive Research Forum (PERF) proposed that police use of force policies should go beyond the *Graham* legal standard of "objective reasonableness." PERF recommends that law enforcement organizations adopt policies to hold themselves to a higher standard, based on sound tactics, consideration of whether the use of force was proportional to the threat, and the sanctity of human life. Training is offered by PERF on critical thinking, crisis intervention, communication, and tactics aimed at developing a new approach toward use of force, and numerous local law enforcement agencies are adopting the PERF recommended use of force standard.

use of force in that jurisdiction, including a requirement that time, distance, and shielding or other de-escalation efforts be made before force is used when feasible.

Tennessee v. Garner, 471 U.S. 1 (1985): Under the Fourth Amendment, a police officer pursuing a fleeing suspect can use deadly force to prevent escape only if "the officer has probable cause to believe that the suspect poses a threat of serious physical harm, either to the officer or to others." The *Garner* decision has been applied in later cases involving a variety of incidents, including vehicle pursuits. Because of the risk to innocent bystanders posed by a high speed police chase, many departments are limiting the situations in which such pursuits are authorized. A use of deadly force complaint involving a fleeing suspect should be closely analyzed in light of *Garner*, subsequent legal decisions, and departmental policies.

2. Stops, Searches, and In-Custody Questioning

Terry v. Ohio, 392 U.S. 1 (1968): The *Terry* stop is a brief investigative detention of an individual to confirm or deny whether the suspect is involved in criminal activity. A *Terry* stop constitutes a seizure under the Fourth Amendment, and the officer must be able to articulate specific facts supporting a reasonable suspicion that "criminal activity may be afoot." If the detention involves a pat-down of outer clothing, a "stop and frisk," the officer also must have articulable reasonable suspicion that the person detained may be armed and pose a danger to the officer or others. An example of factors that taken together could support a *Terry* stop include detaining individuals at 2:00 a.m. in a high drug trafficking area after observing hand-to-hand movement between them. If the detained individuals refuse to keep their hands in plain view and their clothing allows for concealment of weapons or there is a noticeable bulge consistent with a concealed weapon, the officer may be able to articulate a reasonable fear for their safety, justifying a frisk.

While case law varies around the country, examples of circumstances that can contribute to turning a *Terry* stop into a custodial arrest include detaining a person longer than required to investigate the reason for the stop, handcuffing a suspect, drawing and pointing a weapon, or moving an individual to a patrol car for questioning. If an investigative detention becomes an arrest (or is later interpreted to be an arrest), there must be "probable cause," the Fourth Amendment requirement that there is a reasonable basis to believe the detained individual committed a crime.

A CHALLENGE TO NYPD'S STOP AND FRISK PRACTICES

The case of *Floyd et al. v. City of New York et al.*, 959 F. Supp. 2d 540 (2013), provides a good example of why it is important for investigative offices to be familiar with legal developments within their particular jurisdiction. In *Floyd*, the Center for Constitutional Rights challenged the New York Police Department's (NYPD) stop and frisk practices. The case focused on the lack of reasonable suspicion to make these stops and on the racial disparities in who was stopped and searched—approximately 85% of those stopped were blacks or Hispanics, even though these two groups make up only 52% of the city's population. A federal judge found the NYPD liable for a pattern and practice of racial profiling and unconstitutional stops. New York City appealed, but later agreed to drop its challenge and began the court ordered process to modify stop and frisk practices that had been in use. As of December 2019, the court-appointed monitor reported overall improvement in the constitutionality of stops and that the rate of justified frisks had improved. However, the monitor also noted that the percentage of stops meeting constitutional standards continued to be significantly lower for stops of blacks and Hispanics.[1]

As law enforcement tactics have responded to technological advancements, there have been related issues on permissible searches. For example, case law under the Fourth Amendment has established limited exceptions to the search warrant requirement, including a search incident to arrest where protecting officer safety or preventing destruction of evidence is at issue. However, the U.S. Supreme Court has held that law enforcement officers generally are not permitted to search a cell phone incident to arrest without a warrant. *Riley v. California*, 134 S. Ct. 2473 (2014). Another example of the Court addressing the warrant requirement is seen in *Carpenter v. United States*, where FBI agents obtained six months of mobile phone location data from Carpenter's cellular carrier, proving he was in the vicinity of robberies for which he was a suspect. Carpenter argued that the evidence and his subsequent conviction should be thrown out, since law enforcement did not get a warrant for the records. The Supreme Court agreed and ruled that police must obtain a search warrant supported by probable cause before obtaining location data from cellular phone carriers. *Carpenter v. United States*, ___U.S.___, 138 S.Ct. 2206 (2018).

Miranda v. Arizona, 384 U.S. 436 (1966): Before questioning a suspect in custody, police must provide the *Miranda* warning advising the right to remain silent—that anything said can and will be used against them in a court of law, consult with an attorney and have the attorney present during questioning, and have an attorney appointed, if indigent. When a formal arrest has not been made, determining the exact point when police officers have taken someone into custody can be difficult. For purposes of *Miranda*, an objective analysis is conducted to determine if a suspect is "in custody" by considering the circumstances surrounding the questioning and, in light of the circumstances, whether a reasonable person would have felt they were at liberty to end the interrogation and leave. *Thompson v. Keohane*, 516 U.S. 99 (1995).

Though the *Miranda* decision itself has been reaffirmed, there are other cases limiting its scope in certain police operations. A misconduct allegation involving a *Miranda* warning should be carefully analyzed, taking into account the factual circumstances and relevant decisions subsequent to *Miranda*. Failure to properly follow *Miranda* may result in an administrative complaint of officer misconduct and suppression of the suspect's statement during criminal proceedings.

LAW ENFORCEMENT QUESTIONING OF JUVENILES

Juveniles, like adults, must be notified of their *Miranda* rights prior to being interrogated while in custody. In the case of juveniles, however, police officers must take a person's age into account when deciding whether the circumstances merit a *Miranda* warning. *J.D.B. v. North Carolina*, 564. U.S. 261 (2011). In the *J.D.B.* case, a 13-year-old boy who was possibly linked to two burglaries was removed from his classroom by a uniformed police officer, taken to a closed-door conference room and, with two officers and two school administrators present, was questioned for at least 30 to 45 minutes. The 13-year-old was not given the *Miranda* warning, was not given the opportunity to contact his guardian, and was not informed he was free to leave. After the boy admitted to his participation in the burglaries, an officer told him he could refuse to answer questions and leave whenever he wanted, though he stayed and provided further information. The Supreme Court held that the trial court improperly denied the boy's request to throw out his statements and should reconsider, and include the child's age in the analysis of whether he was "in custody."

3. *Misconduct Complaint Investigation Procedures*

Garrity v. New Jersey, 385 U.S. 493 (1967): The Supreme Court held that an officer cannot be compelled by the threat of serious discipline to make statements that may be used in a subsequent criminal proceeding. If an officer's statement is protected from disclosure in a criminal prosecution and the officer receives a *Garrity* advisement, the officer can be compelled to provide an administrative statement without waiving their right against self-incrimination in the criminal context. An officer's statement made after receiving a *Garrity* advisement may be used for administrative investigation purposes, and refusal to provide a statement after a *Garrity* advisement can be grounds for termination. See Chapter 3.C.4. for additional discussion about *Garrity* issues.

Again, it is vital that misconduct complaint investigators understand applicable law in their state or local jurisdiction. For example, in some jurisdictions even if a *Garrity* protected compelled statement is withheld from the prosecutor, a court might consider whether the statement was used in the administrative investigation in ways that could taint other evidence available in the criminal prosecution. See, for example, *Criswell v. State of Indiana*, 02A03–1501-CR-22 (Ind. Ct.App. 2015).

NLRB v. Weingarten, 420 U.S. 251 (1975): An employee who belongs to a union has the right to union representation during any investigatory interview that could lead to discipline of that employee. An investigatory interview is a meeting with management (or a management delegate) at which the employee is questioned or asked to explain his or her conduct, and could lead to discipline. Because misconduct investigations can lead to discipline of a named officer, and investigators are given authority to question the officer, named officers generally are allowed to bring representatives to administrative investigation interviews. Representation rights for both named and witness officers may be spelled out further in jurisdictional law or collective bargaining agreements.

Loudermill v. Cleveland Board of Education, 470 U.S. 532 (1985): Under Fourteenth Amendment due process rights, public sector employees, including law enforcement personnel, are entitled to "some form" of a hearing before they are terminated. A full evidentiary hearing is not required, but the employer must provide the employee with an opportunity to be heard and review the evidence to ensure it supports the outcome. The right to a *Loudermill* hearing, under certain circumstances, may extend to a probationary employee and cases in which significant discipline less than termination is involved, such as demotion or unpaid suspension. Thus, some types of discipline will require a hearing before the matter is finalized.

4. Disclosure of Investigation Materials for Criminal Proceedings

Brady v. Maryland, 373 U.S. 83 (1963): *Brady* requires prosecutors to disclose to the defense materially exculpatory evidence in the government's possession. Material required to be disclosed includes evidence that goes toward negating a defendant's guilt, would reduce a defendant's potential sentence, or diminishes the credibility of a witness. Evidence related to certain types of complaints, such as a sustained finding of dishonesty against an officer who will testify in the criminal case at issue, must be produced under *Brady* as potential impeachment material.

Investigative offices should work with legal counsel to develop clear policies with prosecutors as to when the office may or must share evidence gathered through the misconduct investigation process. For example, in *Association for Los Angeles Deputy Sheriffs v. Superior Court*, 447 P.3d 237 (2019), the California Supreme Court held that confidentiality requirements for certain law enforcement personnel information should be interpreted to allow law enforcement agencies to comply with *Brady* obligations by providing *Brady* alerts to prosecutors. However, the decision did not resolve the question of whether there are mandatory *Brady* requirements that override officers' confidentiality protections.

Review Questions

1. List the various stakeholders who have an interest in the work of an investigative office and discuss reasons why training in stakeholder engagement is important.
2. What are some pros and cons of attending complaint investigation training sponsored by police affiliated organizations verses training offered by groups not affiliated with law enforcement?
3. Outline the *Graham* requirements under the Fourth Amendment for assessing the reasonableness of use of force and provide examples of changes in use of force standards that have been recommended or adopted.
4. Discuss the *Garrity* decision and the role a *Garrity* advisement plays in misconduct complaint investigations.
5. How might investigative offices be implicated in *Brady* requirements for prosecutors?

Note

1 Center for Constitutional Rights, https://ccrjustice.org/home/what-we-do/our-cases/floyd-et-al-v-city-new-york-et-al; and *Tenth Report of the Independent Monitor, Peter L. Zimroth* (December 16, 2019), https://ccrjustice.org/sites/default/files/attach/2019/12/Tenth%20Report%20of%20Floyd%20Monitor%2012-16-19.pdf

In Chapter 8

Administrative Operations

A. Information About the Investigative Office and Accessibility
B. Stakeholder Outreach
C. Confidentiality
D. Conflict of Interest
E. Code of Ethics and Unbiased Treatment
F. Non-Retaliation
G. Organizing and Securing Complaint Files and Documentation
H. Retention and Public Disclosure of Complaint Files
I. Legal Counsel
J. Investigative Office Evaluations

Chapter 8

Administrative Operations

An investigative office handling complaints of police misconduct will need to maintain an infrastructure and procedures to ensure it is accessible to community members and law enforcement personnel, confidential information is protected, and files are secure and well managed. It is very important that communications with all individuals having contact with the investigative office convey concern for and commitment to those served. Whether contact is by telephone, in the reception area, in an interview setting, or otherwise, the perception of the agency will be influenced either positively or negatively by each encounter. Professionalism, civility, and compassion, especially in difficult or challenging situations, should be expected of all personnel.

DEVELOP A MISSION STATEMENT

A mission statement that describes the purpose and goals of the investigative office should be developed. A well-written mission statement will inform community members and the law enforcement department about the values of the office in conducting its work, and can provide inspiration to investigative staff.

A. Information About the Investigative Office and Accessibility

Basic information describing the investigative office and its authority, how to file a complaint, and any deadlines involved should be available through a number of different media, such as the investigative office and law enforcement agency websites, brochures, and posters throughout the community and in the police department, including holding cell areas. Examples of useful information to include in publications or on the website include:

- Description of the types of issues handled by the investigative office, how to file a complaint or compliment, and an overview of the investigative process, including timelines.
- Complaint and compliment forms—electronic and downloadable—as well as details of where to obtain hard copies.
- Description of any mediation or other alternative dispute resolution options.
- Hours of operation, investigative office address and directions, and telephone number.
- Frequently asked questions (FAQs).

- Links to:
  - o Policies and procedures for the investigative office.
  - o The law enforcement department policy manual.
  - o Applicable collective bargaining agreements.
  - o Information about any independent police oversight agency in the jurisdiction, including the enabling legislation (if different from the investigative office).
  - o An advisory to complainants and named officers of the right to consult an attorney or union representative before providing a statement.
  - o Investigative office reports and recommendations.
  - o Information concerning specific cases or hearings, as permitted.
  - o Outreach brochures and similar documents.
  - o Investigative office social media accounts.
  - o Complaint investigation evaluation form—electronic and downloadable—as well as details of where to obtain hard copies.

Investigative offices must ensure that they are readily accessible to all, including people with disabilities. As a public entity, the investigative office should maintain standards of accessibility and offer accommodations as needed, such as being prepared to communicate with someone who is hearing impaired through TTY (Text Telephone) or TDD (Telecommunication Device for the Deaf). There are many resources available at the federal, state, and local levels when considering how to best welcome and accommodate individuals with disabilities.[1]

Investigative offices should also consider arranging for translators or developing other resources to communicate with non-English speaking members of the community. Individuals who are not fluent English speakers may need an interpreter to complete a complaint form, communicate with the investigative office by phone, participate in an interview, or for other reasons. Basic information about the office should be translated into the most commonly used languages in the jurisdiction and be posted on the website and available for distribution.

B. Stakeholder Outreach

In addition to widely distributing materials about the work of the investigative office and maintaining an informative website, there should be ongoing outreach. Some important constituents with whom the investigative office should regularly meet include:

- Community groups, ethnic, cultural, and faith-based organizations, business associations, and other community stakeholders.
- Line officers, supervisors, command staff, union representatives, and other departmental employee groups.
- Government officials.
- Youth, through "know your rights and responsibilities" publications and workshops in schools, youth organizations, and juvenile detention facilities.[2]
- Criminal prosecution and defense attorneys, civil rights organizations, and similar groups.

Outreach through press releases, interviews, or talk shows with local media, including print publications, radio, podcasts, and television, should be arranged routinely, when significant reports are issued by the investigative office, or if there is a community concern that should be addressed.

Disseminating information about the work of the investigative office and a commitment to continual process improvement, will help promote a reputation for accountability and transparency.

C. Confidentiality

All investigative office personnel should be mindful of jurisdictional law and police agency policy that applies to confidentiality of police misconduct complaint information, including the identity of the parties and witnesses involved. Some jurisdictions prohibit any disclosure of complaint information, some allow for the disclosure of information only for those cases in which allegations are sustained against an officer, while other jurisdictions strive toward broader transparency and allow more information to be made public (except where the rights of victims of crimes, minors, or others are implicated).

Regardless of the jurisdictional rules, it is best practice to keep the identity of the parties and other particulars of a complaint confidential during the pendency of an investigation. Publicizing complaint details while an investigation is in process can interfere with the investigation, lead to speculation about the outcome, or could dissuade witnesses from coming forward out of fear of publicity or retaliation.

Require investigative office personnel to sign a confidentiality agreement that spells out the specific legal and policy mandates that apply. There also should be a clear protocol to address unique situations when it might be more difficult to protect confidentiality, such as in responding to media inquiries when the identity of the parties is already public information.

D. Conflict of Interest

Investigative offices should establish conflict of interest policies and procedures, requiring that personnel who become aware of an actual or apparent conflict of interest with anyone involved with the complaint to immediately bring the issue to the attention of management. The fact that a staff member might have previously worked with or had other contact with the complainant, involved officer, or a witness does not automatically create a conflict. However, if any previous work experience or other relationship with anyone concerned might impact (or have the appearance of impacting) neutrality in handling the investigation, the issue should be reviewed with management, for reassignment or possible referral outside of the office.

E. Code of Ethics and Unbiased Treatment

Developing a code of ethics for the investigative office reinforces the serious nature of the work and sets behavioral standards that will help promote public trust and legitimacy for investigations handled by the office. Principles typically addressed include, all investigative office personnel must conduct themselves in a professional, fair, and impartial manner, investigations will be handled diligently, thoroughly, and objectively, and all individuals should be treated with dignity and respect.

While biased policing allegations are discussed in Chapter 5.E., consideration also should be given to the issue of how implicit bias can impact the work of investigators, individuals reviewing investigations, and those making final determinations on the allegations involved.[3] Being mindful of subtle ways prejudices and stereotypes can influence the process is vital, and implicit bias training is recommended for all employees involved in the complaint investigation process.

F. Non-Retaliation

Investigative office personnel should work to prevent retaliation against anyone involved in the investigative process. Fear of retaliation can dissuade members of the public or police officers from filing complaints or providing testimony. While an investigative office may have contact with criminal investigators or prosecutors when there are pending criminal charges against the complainant or named officer, investigators must avoid real or perceived retaliation in those communications. Though filing a complaint does not create a safe harbor against criminal processes, investigative offices should establish protocols and admonishments for employees to avoid even the appearance of improper contact. The issue of alleged retaliation by police officers against complainants is discussed in Chapter 2 (see textbox "Retaliation Should Be Explicitly Prohibited").

G. Organizing and Securing Complaint Files and Documentation

Investigative files, physical evidence, and other investigative office records should be kept secure. Procedures should be developed to establish hard copy and/or electronic filing systems, with protocols to specify who should have access, how to maintain file security, and how to protect the integrity of files if they are removed from the secured filing area or investigative office.

All complaints should be sequentially numbered by year, regardless of the seriousness or merit of the allegation made or how the matter will be investigated or resolved, with a ready means for cross-reference and searches. Investigative files should follow the same organizational format to facilitate the research and review process. For discussion about tracking complaints and building a complete database, see Chapter 4.I. and Chapter 6.

H. Retention and Public Disclosure of Complaint Files

Record retention laws and policies vary by jurisdiction and should guide the agency in creating procedures for file storage and destruction. Protocols should be developed to routinely (at least annually) audit investigative files to determine if any are missing, which should be retained, and which should be purged. Unless retention is prohibited, there may be historical and evidentiary value in retaining complaint records, though it can create storage problems and greatly complicate a search for documents in responding to discovery, public disclosure requests, and other inquiries.

Requirements regarding access to investigations and related information through public disclosure processes differ by jurisdiction. Protocols should be in place for handling information requests, addressing such issues as: the staff position responsible for responding, time limits, the scope of any search for information in response to a request, exemption and redaction rules, and the responsibility for costs involved.

I. Legal Counsel

The need to consult with legal counsel may arise at various points throughout the investigation process, as noted in earlier chapters. Counsel should update investigative office staff routinely about relevant changes in the law, police department policies, and collective bargaining contracts. It also may be helpful to consult legal counsel when:

- There are legal questions about substantive issues being investigated or the investigative process itself.
- There are questions concerning an administrative investigation related to a criminal charge against the named officer.
- A proceeding under the collective bargaining contract (such as a grievance) is initiated implicating the investigative agency.
- The office receives a public disclosure request, subpoena, or discovery request initiated in a criminal or civil litigation matter for files or testimony from agency personnel concerning an investigation or other investigative office matters.
- The investigative office has obligations to provide investigation information pursuant to *Brady*.
- An investigative office develops policies on retention and destruction of misconduct investigation files.

J. Investigative Office Evaluations

During the process of administratively closing a case, it is useful to seek feedback from the parties about their experience with the investigative office. An evaluation can be included with the closure notice and should be available on-line, with the parties encouraged to submit information to help the office improve its services. The evaluation form should not require that the parties identify themselves or the case number to allow for anonymous responses.

Evaluations are an important tool the investigative office and its stakeholders can use to assess and improve operations and effectiveness. Summary information about lessons learned from evaluations should be included in public reports.

Review Questions

1. Specify some reasons as to why it is necessary to keep complaint information confidential.
2. What are ways of informing the community and other stakeholders about the work of the investigative office? Why is it important to do outreach?
3. How might a code of ethics be relevant to an investigative office? In what ways can bias affect investigations?
4. Discuss why it is important for a non-retaliation policy to be included in information that an investigative office distributes to the community.

Notes

1 See, for example, *Information and Technical Assistance on the Americans with Disabilities Act*, www.ada.gov/index.html

2 For an example of an informative outreach publication prepared for youth by the San Jose Independent Police Auditor, see *A Student's Guide to Police Practices*, https://www.sanjoseca.gov/your-government/appointees/independent-police-auditor/publications/student-guide

3 See Tracy G. Gove, "Implicit Bias and Law Enforcement," *The Police Chief* 78 (October 2011): 44–66.

In Chapter 9

Civilian Oversight of Law Enforcement

A. Oversight in the United States
B. Models and Functions of Oversight
C. Components Contributing to Successful Oversight
   1. Independent and Diverse
   2. Political Will—Support of and Access to Government Officials
   3. Ample Authority
   4. Adequate Funding
   5. Training and Qualifications for Effective Oversight
   6. Garnering Community/Stakeholder Support and Outreach
D. Research on Civilian Oversight and Complaint Investigations
E. The National Association for Civilian Oversight of Law Enforcement (NACOLE)
   1. Core Competencies
   2. Code of Ethics
   3. NACOLE Credential and Qualification Standards

Chapter 9

Civilian Oversight of Law Enforcement

Heightened attention to law enforcement activities and the broader criminal justice system in recent years has led to reforms and a call for greater community input. Many see civilian oversight of law enforcement as a means to improve law enforcement practices and police–community relations. In 2015, the President's Task Force on 21st Century Policing noted that, "some form of civilian oversight is important in order to strengthen trust with the community."[1] Civilian oversight programs with ample authority and resources can contribute to the accountability, transparency, and legitimacy of law enforcement. Oversight works to ensure that the priorities and practices of law enforcement agencies are in keeping with community values and can help restore or improve public confidence in policing.

A. Oversight in the United States

Until the 20th century, city mayors, acting alone or in conjunction with politically appointed police commissions, were responsible for overseeing law enforcement. Police commissions had varied responsibilities and their members served at the pleasure of the appointing authority, with expectations of loyalty to the executive and the police department. As oversight has evolved since the 1970s, new approaches to police accountability have brought community perspective and independence to the oversight function.

Oversight in a particular jurisdiction may be established as a means to address recurring law enforcement problems or in response to a single high profile police incident. In some cases, jurisdictions have proactively developed oversight to enhance police–community relations.

Oversight has become an integral part of municipal administrations in most large cities in the U.S., with some smaller cities and counties also developing mechanisms for community members to weigh in on police matters. Increasingly, oversight programs also are being developed for prisons, jails, and other detention facilities. Non-governmental organizations, such as the American Civil Liberties Union, the National Association for the Advancement of Colored People, and the Southern Poverty Law Center, also work to enhance accountability in law enforcement, while governmental agencies, such as the Department of Justice, work to ensure constitutional practices throughout the criminal justice system. In addition, inspector generals and other entities provide oversight at the federal level, addressing misconduct and promoting integrity among federal law enforcement and other federal personnel.

NATIONAL ASSOCIATION FOR CIVILIAN OVERSIGHT OF LAW ENFORCEMENT (NACOLE)

NACOLE is an organization that works to establish or improve oversight in the U.S. The NACOLE website lists and provides links to approximately 140 oversight agencies throughout the country, along with detailed profiles of a sample group of those organizations. As discussed throughout this chapter, NACOLE provides training and other support for oversight agencies, as detailed on its website.

B. Models and Functions of Oversight

Civilian oversight organizations in the U.S. include a variety of different structures or models, such as commissions, boards, inspector generals, auditors, monitors, and investigative agencies. Oversight agencies use labels interchangeably, and many are "hybrids" incorporating multiple functions regardless of the title. Oversight programs may have authority to function in any or all of the following capacities:

- Accepting and referring misconduct complaints
- Investigating misconduct complaints
- Monitoring or auditing a department's internal investigations and findings
- Recommend findings and discipline
- Conducting hearings and making decisions on discipline matters
- Conducting systemic reviews
- Making recommendations for improving policies, practices, and training
- Reporting on oversight and its impact
- Fostering community education and engagement about law enforcement and oversight matters

Most oversight organizations are multifaceted and work to improve policing and police–community relations in a variety of different ways. Oversight is not a static process and functions may be evaluated and changed over time to improve practices and to be continually responsive to changing community needs.

C. Components Contributing to Successful Oversight

Regardless of the oversight structure set up in a particular jurisdiction, there are a number of factors that contribute to whether an approach will be successful. The components outlined here should be considered in adopting oversight at the outset or as changes are contemplated.

1. Independent and Diverse

In order to succeed, the oversight body must be independent from special interest groups, police, and elected and other government officials. Community members and law enforcement must be confident that the oversight agency and its leadership are fair and unbiased, in order to see its work as legitimate. The oversight body and leadership should not be censored in making findings or issuing public reports within the established authority of the agency. Staff and members of boards and commissions should reflect the jurisdiction served.

2. *Political Will—Support of and Access to Government Officials*

The backing of government officials who value independence, accountability, and transparency is necessary for effective oversight. It is important for the integration of the oversight agency into the government structure that oversight practitioners have direct access to elected and other government officials. Government officials must support the independence of the oversight function, findings, and recommendations.

3. *Ample Authority*

It is imperative that oversight organizations have ample authority to provide a credible service to the communities they serve. For example, agencies that have investigative authority must have the ability to interview witnesses, including officers, and have access (via subpoena power or otherwise) to incident-related documents, video/audio recordings, and other evidence needed to complete their investigations. Similarly, agencies that audit or monitor investigations conducted by an internal police division must have the power to correct deficient investigations by requiring further inquiry or conducting an independent investigation themselves. All oversight organizations should have the ability to make recommendations about ways to improve police policies, practices, and training when deficiencies become apparent.

4. *Adequate Funding*

Oversight programs must have adequate funding to complete the work outlined in the enabling legislation. Oversight agencies that investigate, audit, or monitor complaints must have funding to hire professional staff to manage and conduct investigations thoroughly and in a timely manner, to prepare reports, to respond to litigation discovery and requests for public disclosure, and for other purposes. The costs of purchasing a database program to track all aspects of the process may be steep, but a tracking system is vital to the mission of the agency, particularly in large organizations. Some agencies have budgets derived from staffing ratios with the law enforcement organization written into the enabling legislation.

5. *Training and Qualifications for Effective Oversight*

In order to be effective and legitimate in conducting law enforcement oversight, practitioners and volunteers must have the training and experience to perform high-quality unbiased work. NACOLE is an important training resource for those involved in oversight; additional training resources and other specific training topics are discussed in Chapter 7. In addition, attending academy classes or other law enforcement sponsored training can provide insight for oversight staff about the work of policing; interacting in these classes also can help officers better understand the role of oversight, thereby increasing oversight legitimacy. Participating in structured ride-alongs and shadowing police personnel in units throughout the law enforcement department is strongly recommended.

6. Garnering Community/Stakeholder Support and Outreach

It is important that oversight offices keep all stakeholders informed of the services and work of the agency through its website, outreach, social media, published reports, and other methods of communication. Educational outreach should also clarify the limitations of the authority of the oversight agency to help manage community expectations. Outreach is discussed further in Chapter 8.B.

D. Research on Civilian Oversight and Complaint Investigations

While civilian oversight of law enforcement has been in existence in a variety of forms across the U.S. for many years, there is a limited body of independent empirical research evaluating the impact of different oversight models. NACOLE and the Office of Justice Programs (OJP) Diagnostic Center sponsored a study published in 2016 that assessed the research available on oversight and provided recommendations for future study.[2] Among the recommendations made were suggestions that there be an assessment of impacts of oversight on public trust and confidence in law enforcement, more standardization in reporting and measurements across oversight agencies, and support for oversight research from organizations currently supporting law enforcement studies.

An example of current research is a survey of oversight agencies being conducted by NACOLE to study the state of the field and effective practices in oversight through a grant received from the U.S. Department of Justice, Community Oriented Policing Services (COPS). Other options available to individual agencies to assess program effectiveness include:

- Peer review to obtain input on agency service quality and organizational integrity. NACOLE has expertise to help facilitate peer review.
- Partnerships with academic institutions to study the impact of their program and to develop strategies for organizational excellence.

E. The National Association for Civilian Oversight of Law Enforcement (NACOLE)

NACOLE is the professional development and support organization for those involved in oversight and has worked to establish standards and training for oversight practitioners at all levels. The organization provides annual and regional training and networking conferences for those committed to police accountability including law enforcement and government officials, oversight practitioners, and the general public.

1. Core Competencies

In support of its training program for oversight professionals, NACOLE has developed a set of six core competencies that are central to effective oversight: (1) the history, theories, and models of oversight; (2) skills and techniques for conducting or auditing complaint investigations; (3) informing the public and transparency, including outreach and reporting; (4) relevant law and ethics of law enforcement and oversight; (5) law enforcement policies and procedures; and (6) remediation and discipline, including mediation, early warning systems, Education Based Discipline, and the appellate process.

2. Code of Ethics

NACOLE has developed a code of ethics that can be adopted in whole or used as a guide for an oversight agency as it develops its own standards. The NACOLE Code of Ethics covers a number of principles important to any investigative office, whether internal or external to law enforcement, many of which are addressed throughout the *Complaint Investigations Manual.*

3. NACOLE Credential and Qualification Standards

In addition to conferences and regional meetings, the NACOLE Certified Practitioner of Oversight (CPO) Credential Program recognizes oversight practitioners who have completed pre-approved hours of training offered at NACOLE conferences and webinars. Maintaining the credential requires ongoing education.

NACOLE has also developed recommended qualification standards for individuals handling police misconduct complaints, including investigators, supervisors, and executive personnel (directors, inspectors general, auditors, and monitors), as well as training suggestions for appointed board and commission members. While unique factors relating to the work of a particular oversight agency may indicate the need for personnel with other specific experience, NACOLE's "Qualification Standards for Oversight Agencies" serves as a convenient reference tool.[3]

Review Questions

1. What are the potential benefits of developing law enforcement oversight programs?
2. Discuss some of the models and functions of oversight programs.
3. Name some of the components that contribute to oversight being successful in conducting its work. Why are these components important?

Notes

1 President's Task Force on 21st Century Policing, *Final Report of the President's Task Force on 21st Century Policing* (Office of Community Oriented Policing Services, 2015), Recommendation 2.8.

2 Joseph De Angelis, Richard Rosenthal, and Brian Buchner, *Civilian Oversight of Law Enforcement: Assessing the Evidence* (Office of Justice Programs Diagnostic Center, U.S. Department of Justice, October 2016).

3 *Qualification Standards for Oversight Investigators*, nacole.org/qualification_standards_for_oversight_agencies

Chapter 10

Conclusion

Investigations of misconduct complaints must be conducted with an open mind and sense of determination to establish the facts of the underlying incident. The *Complaint Investigations Manual* is a starting place—actually doing qualitative investigative work requires training, experience, and a positive attitude toward feedback. Those handling police misconduct complaints can gain the trust of the community and law enforcement by earning a reputation for being fair, thorough, impartial, and timely in their work.

Investigations of police misconduct complaints involve complicated issues that require an in-depth understanding of applicable federal and state law, law enforcement policies and practices, and collective bargaining contracts. Investigative offices should create systems to effectively and efficiently receive, classify, and investigate complaints. Procedures must be in place to ensure that investigations are thorough and timely, and that evidence collected is analyzed without bias and in the context of the law and policies that apply. The findings and recommendations that result should be objective, based on the evidence collected, and difficult credibility determinations may be involved. To ensure that the staff is well versed and consistent in all of these areas, investigative offices should have training programs and supervision systems in place.

The *Manual* is intended as a sourcebook for all who investigate, review, or evaluate police misconduct matters. Whether investigations are conducted internally, or by an independent oversight authority, the principles and concepts of good investigations are universal. Whether working in an investigative office that handles thousands of misconduct allegations each year or a smaller jurisdiction with relatively few complaints, investigative personnel must be committed to the values of accountability and transparency, helping to ensure that law enforcement efforts are professional, constitutional, and respect the values of the community served. The *Complaint Investigations Manual* was written to serve these goals.

References

Aronie, Jonathan, and Christy E. Lopez. "Keeping Each Other Safe: An Assessment of the Use of Peer Intervention Programs to Prevent Police Officer Mistakes and Misconduct, Using New Orleans' EPIC Program as a Potential National Mode." *Police Quarterly* 20(3) (September 2017): 295–321.

Association of Workplace Investigators. *Guiding Principles for Conducting Workplace Investigations* (2014). https://www.awi.org/page/Guiding_Principles

Attard, Barbara. *In Praise of Mediation* (1999). http://www.accountabilityassociates.org/publications

Attard, Barbara. "Oversight of Law Enforcement is Beneficial and Needed—Both Inside and Out." *Pace Law Review* 30 (2010): 1548–61.

Attorney General Law Enforcement Directive No. 2019-3. Law Enforcement Interactions with Transgender Individuals (November 20, 2019). https://www.nj.gov/oag/dcj/directiv.htm

Batts, Anthony W., Sean Michael Smoot, and Ellen Scrivner. "Police Leadership Challenges in a Changing World." *New Perspectives in Policing Bulletin*. U.S. Department of Justice, National Institute of Justice (2012). NCJ 238338.

Bibring, Peter, Matthew Cagle, Chris Conley, Mitra Ebadolahi, Jessica Farris, Linda Lye, and Nicole Ozer. *Making Smart Decisions About Surveillance: A Guide for Community Transparency, Accountability, and Oversight*. The ACLU of California (April 2016). https://www.aclunc.org/publications/making-smart-decisions-about-surveillance-guide-community-transparency-accountability

Brenneke, Andrea. "A Restorative Circle in the Wake of a Police Shooting." *Tikkun Magazine* 27(1) (2012).

Browne, Michael K., and Ryan Patrick. "Coaching by Police Supervisors: Civilian Oversight Innovation Impacts Police Performance." *NACOLE Review* (Summer 2014): 4.

Charlotte-Mecklenburg Police. *Employee Conduct: Investigations & Discipline—A Guidebook for the Public and Our Employees on What We Do and Why We Do It* (2005).

Colaprete, Frank A. *Internal Investigations—A Practitioner's Approach*. Charles C. Thomas (2007).

Commission on Accreditation for Law Enforcement Agencies. *CALEA Standards for Law Enforcement Agencies* (2006).

De Angelis, Joseph, Richard Rosenthal, and Brian Buchner. *Civilian Oversight of Law Enforcement: Assessing the Evidence*. Office of Justice Programs Diagnostic Center, U.S. Department of Justice (October 2016).

Dekmar, Louis M. "Handling Citizen Complaints Through Proactive Methodology." *The Police Chief* 77 (April 2010): 50–52.

Department of Justice Report on Investigation of the Ferguson Police Department (March 4, 2015). https://www.justice.gov/sites/default/files/opa/press-releases/attachments/2015/03/04/ferguson_police_department_report.pdf

Department of Justice Report Regarding the Criminal Investigation into the Shooting Death of Michael Brown by Ferguson, Missouri Police Officer Darren Wilson (March 4, 2015). https://www.justice.gov/sites/default/files/opa/press-releases/attachments/2015/03/04/doj_report_on_shooting_of_michael_brown_1.pdf

Ferdik, Frank V., Jeff Rojeck, and Geoffrey P. Alpert. "Citizen Oversight in the United States and Canada: An Overview." *Police Practice and Research: An International Journal* 14(2) (2013): 104–16.

Finn, Peter. *Citizen Review of Police—Approaches and Implementation*. National Institute of Justice Issues and Practices, U.S. Department of Justice, Office of Justice Programs (2001).

Fyfe, James, ed. *Police Management Today: Issues and Case Studies*. International City Management Association (1985).

Gove, Tracy G. "Implicit Bias and Law Enforcement." *The Police Chief* 78 (October 2011): 44–66.

Green, Rodney D., and Jillian Aldebron. "In Search of Police Accountability: Civilian Review Boards and Department of Justice Intervention." *Phylon* 56 (2019): 111–33.

Greenwald, Howard P., and Charlie Beck. "Bringing Sides Together: Community-Based Complaint Mediation." *The Police Chief* 85 (August 2018): 36–42.

Harris, Anna R. "For a Culture of Integrity, Focus on Fairness." *National Defense* (2018). https://www.nationaldefensemagazine.org/articles/2018/1/4/for-a-culture-of-integrity-focus-on-fairness

Hendrickson, Kimberly, and Kathryn Olson. "Introduction." In "Moving Beyond Discipline—The Role of Civilians in Police Accountability." NACOLE/CJPR special issue, *Criminal Justice Policy Review* 27(5) (2015): 1–8.

Hickman, Matthew, and Jane Poore. "National Data on Citizen Complaints About Police Use of Force: Data Quality Concerns and the Potential (Mis)use of Statistical Evidence to Address Police Agency Conduct." *Criminal Justice Policy Review* 27 (2016): 455–79.

International Association of Chiefs of Police. *Protecting Civil Rights: A Leadership Guide for State, Local, and Tribal Law Enforcement* (September 2006).

International Association of Chiefs of Police. *Transparency: Law Enforcement's Best Friend* (July 2012).

International Association of Chiefs of Police, National Law Enforcement Policy Center. *Investigation of Employee Misconduct—Concepts and Issues Paper and Model Policy* (2007).

International Association of Chiefs of Police and U.S. Department of Justice, Office of Community Oriented Policing Services. *Bridging the Trust Gap Between Law Enforcement and Communities of Color Toolkit* (2017).

International Association of Chiefs of Police and U.S. Department of Justice, Office of Community Oriented Policing Services. *Building Trust Between the Police and Citizens They Serve—An Internal Affairs Promising Practices Guide for Local Law Enforcement* (2009).

Jones, Gareth. *Conducting Administrative, Oversight & Ombudsman Investigations*. The Cartwright Group (2009).

Jurado, Ray. "Practice Tips—The Harm to Public Service Standard in Police Misconduct Cases." *Los Angeles Lawyer* (July/August 2005).

Kane, Robert J., and Michael D White. *Jammed Up—Bad Cops, Police Misconduct, and the New York City Police Department*. New York University Press (2013).

Keiling, George L., Robert Wasserman, and Hubert Williams. "Police Accountability and Community Policing." *Perspectives on Policing Bulletin*. U.S. Department of Justice, National Institute of Justice (1988). NCJ 114211.

Kennedy, David M. *Don't Shoot: One Man, a Street Fellowship, and the End of Violence in Inner-City America*. Bloomsbury (2011).

Lee, Heeuk D., Peter A. Collins, Ming-Li Hsieh, Francis D. Boateng, and David Brody. "Officer Attitudes Toward Citizen Review and Professional Accountability." *Police Science and Management* 19(2) (2017): 63–71.

LePard, Doug, and John M. (Jack) Collins. "Showing Incident Video to Police Officers Under Investigation—A Best Practice Approach." *The Police Chief* 82 (March 2015): 20–24.

Los Angeles County Sheriff's Department. *Guidelines for Discipline Handbook*, rev. ed. (January 24, 2017).

Lum, Cynthia, Megan Stoltz, Christopher S. Koper, and J. Amber Scherer. "Research on Body-Worn Cameras—What We Know, What We Need to Know." *Criminology & Public Policy* 18 (2019): 93–118. https://doi.org/10.1111/1745-9133.12412

Luna-Firebaugh, Eileen. *Tribal Policing: Asserting Sovereignty, Seeking Justice*. University of Arizona Press (2007).

Martineli, Thomas J. "Minimizing Risk by Defining Off-Duty Police Misconduct." *The Police Chief* 74 (June 2007).

Mastrofski, Stephen D., Tal Jonathan-Zamir, Shomron Moyal, and James J. Willis. "Predicting Procedural Justice in Police–Citizen Encounters. *Criminal Justice and Behavior* 43 (2016): 119–39.

Meares, Tracey L. "Rightful Policing." *New Perspectives in Policing Bulletin*. U.S. Department of Justice, National Institute of Justice (2015). NJC 248411.

Memon, Amina, Christian A. Meissner, and Joanne Fraser. "The Cognitive Interview: A Meta-Analytic Review and Study Space Analysis of the Past 25 Years." *Psychology, Public Policy, and Law* 16 (2010): 340–72.

Miller, Lindsay, Jessica Toliver, and Police Executive Research Forum. *Implementing a Body-Worn Camera Program: Recommendations and Lessons Learned*. U.S. Department of Justice, Office of Community Oriented Policing Services (2014).

Mouallem, Omar. "Policing the Police." *Alberta Views* (June 2013).

Narr, Tony, Jessica Toliver, Jerry Murphy, Malcolm McFarland, and Joshua Ederheimer. *Police Management of Mass Demonstrations: Identifying Issues and Successful Approaches*. Police Executive Research Forum (2006).

Newkirk, Vann R. "An Alternative to the Madness of Proving Police Injustice." *The Atlantic* (June 2016).

New York City Department of Investigation, Office of the Inspector General for the NYPD. *Addressing Inefficiencies in NYPD's Handling of Complaints: An Investigation of the "Outside Guidelines" Complaint Process* (February 2017).

New York City Department of Investigation, Office of the Inspector General for the NYPD. *Observations on Accountability and Transparency in Ten NYPD Chokehold Cases* (January 2015).

Noble, Jeffrey J., and Geoffrey P. Alpert. *Managing Accountability Systems for Police Conduct: Internal Affairs and External Oversight*. Waveland Press (2009).

Olson, Kathryn, and Barbara Attard. *Overview of Civilian Oversight of Law Enforcement in the United States* (2013). http://www.accountabilityassociates.org/publications

Perino, Justina Cintron, ed. *Citizen Oversight of Law Enforcement*. ABA Publishing (2006).

Police Executive Research Forum. *Civil Rights Investigations of Local Police: Lessons Learned* (July 2013).

Police Executive Research Forum. *Legitimacy and Procedural Justice: A New Element of Police Leadership*. U.S. Department of Justice, Bureau of Justice Assistance (March 2014).

Police Executive Research Forum. *Operational Strategies to Build Police–Community Trust and Reduce Crime in Minority Communities: The Minneapolis Cedar-Riverside Exploratory Policing Study*. U.S. Department of Justice, Bureau of Justice Assistance (2017).

Police Foundation. *5 Things You Need to Know About Analyzing Police Traffic Stop Data*. https://www.policefoundation.org/wp-content/uploads/2017/03/5-Things-on-Analyzing-Police-Traffic-Stop-Data-1.pdf (accessed December 17, 2019).

Ponomarenko, Maria, and Barry Friedman. "Democratic Accountability and Policing." *Reforming Criminal Justice* 2 (2017).

President's Task Force on 21st Century Policing. *Final Report of the President's Task Force on 21st Century Policing*. Office of Community Oriented Policing Services (2015).

Quattlebaum, Megan, Tracey Meares, and Tom Tyler. *Principles of Procedurally Just Policing*. The Justice Collaboratory at Yale Law School (2018).

Quinn, Michael. *The Police Code of Silence: Walking with the Devil—What Bad Cops Don't Want You to Know and Good Cops Won't Tell You*, 2nd ed. Quinn and Associates (2011).

Rahr, Sue, and Stephen K. Rice. "From Warriors to Guardians: Recommitting American Police Culture to Democratic Ideals." *New Perspectives in Policing Bulletin*. U.S. Department of Justice, National Institute of Justice (2015). NCJ 248654.

Reiter, Lou. *Law Enforcement Administrative Investigations*. Legal and Risk Management Institute, Public Agency Training Council (2006).

Report of the Independent Commission on the Los Angeles Police Department (1991). http://michellawyers.com/wp-content/uploads/2010/06/Report-of-the-Independent-Commission-on-the-LAPD-re-Rodney-King_Reduced.pdf

Reuters Investigates. *Shock Tactics: Inside the Taser, the Weapon That Transformed Policing; A Reuters Series* (2017). https://www.reuters.com/investigates/section/usa-taser/

Sastry, Anjuli, and Karen Grigsby Bates. "When LA Erupted in Anger: A Look Back at the Rodney King Riots." *NPR Special Series: The Los Angeles Riots, 25 Years On* (April 26, 2017).

Schuster, Beth. "Police Lineups: Making Eyewitness Identification More Reliable." *NIJ Journal* 258 (October 2007).

Scott, Ian D. *Issues in Civilian Oversight of Policing in Canada*. Canada Law Book (2014).

Skolnick, Jerome, and James Fyfe. *Above the Law: Police and the Excessive Use of Force*. The Free Press (1993).

Stageman, Daniel L., Nicole M. Napolitano, and Brian Buchner. "New Approaches to Data-Driven Civilian Oversight of Law Enforcement: An Introduction to the Second NACOLE/CJPR Special Issue." *Criminal Justice Policy Review* (2016): 1–17.

Stamper, Norm. *To Protect and Serve*. Nation Books (2016).

Standards and Guidelines for Internal Affairs: Recommendations from a Community of Practice. U.S. Department of Justice, Community Oriented Policing Services (August 21, 2009).

Stephens, Darrell W. *Police Discipline: A Case for Change*. U.S. Department of Justice, National Institute of Justice (2011).

Stone, Christopher, and Jeremy Travis. *Toward a New Professionalism in Policing*. U.S. Department of Justice, National Institute of Justice (2011).

Strategic Community Practices: A Toolkit for Police Executives. U.S. Department of Justice, Community Oriented Policing Services (January 2012).

Summary Report of Investigation, Office of Inspector General, Case #15–0564 (Officer Jason Van Dyke) (June 30, 2016). https://news.wttw.com/sites/default/files/article/file-attachments/15-0564%20-%20Van%20Dyke%20Summary%20Report%20FINAL.pdf

Teran, Diana M. "Parallel or Consecutive Investigations: Difficult Choices at the Intersection of Crime and Misconduct." *NACOLE Review* (Summer 2011).

The Paradox of American Policing: Performance without Legitimacy. U.S. Department of Justice, Community Oriented Policing Services (July 2010).

Walker, Sam, and Carol A. Archbold. *The New World of Police Accountability*, 2nd ed. Sage (2014).

Wallentine, Ken. "PDs Don't Accurately Track Use of Force. Here's How They Can." *PoliceOne.com* (March 2016).

Index

Made in United States
Troutdale, OR
06/29/2025

32479780R00066